PROLOGUE

SEED
OF THE
FUTURE

SOME THINGS YOU HAVE TO TAKE ON FAITH, even when you know it's based on the more rigid discipline of science. I was holding the cone of a giant sequoia in my hand. It was the size of a hen's egg—a *small* hen's egg, the size I might pass over in the grocery store if I saw a dozen of them, thinking them too puny to fry or scramble for a decent breakfast. Dean Shenk, a park ranger at the Mariposa Grove in Yosemite National Park, reached over and tapped the cone a few times with his index finger. There were still a few seeds in it, and they collected in the bowl of my palm like tiny flecks of dry skin. One seed by itself would hardly be noticeable. On the tip of my finger, it was just a speck.

Then Shenk invited me to look up from that speck to the tree looming behind him: the Grizzly Giant, the rock-star attraction of the Mariposa Grove, once thought to be the oldest and biggest sequoia in the area, before advances in the study of *Sequoiadendron giganteum* (you don't have to know Latin to understand this is a species of something very large) knocked it down a peg or two. The Grizzly Giant is now believed to be about two thousand years old (versus three thousand, as originally thought) and is ranked second by volume in the grove to the Washington Tree and just out of the top twenty-five by volume of all giant sequoias. It's only 64 percent the size of Sequoia National Park's General Sherman Tree, the most massive living tree on the planet.

Still, regardless of any slippage in the rankings, the Grizzly Giant is a monster of a tree—209 feet tall, 92.5 feet in circumference, and 29.5 feet in

Each sequoia cone, the size of a hen's egg, contains two hundred seeds.

diameter at the base, an estimated 34,005 cubic feet in volume. If the tree were a one-story storage room with an 8-foot ceiling, its other dimensions would be 42.5 feet by 100 feet. It has a *branch*, thrusting out from the trunk high above the ground, that is 7 feet in diameter, more massive by itself than most trees, yet just one of many appendages to a living organism whose size beggars the imagination, and whose age stretches back two millennia to the time when Caesar Augustus ordered all the world to be taxed.

The Grizzly Giant, Shenk wanted me to understand, was once a single seed like the speck on my fingertip. Everything the Grizzly Giant has become—all of its stupendous size, all of its monumental longevity—had once been enclosed in something that might be mistaken for a flake of dan-

druff. From little seeds, mighty things can grow and become nearly immortal. I believed him, but understanding, *truly* understanding? That required some faith. The leap from minuscule seed to gigantic tree was so immense; the contemplation of so much time elapsing while the seed emerged from the soil and grew to maturity, as human history passed from the Iron Age to the Space Age, was too dizzying. (Adding to my imaginative vertigo was the realization that, according to the accepted actuarial tables of sequoias, with a little luck the Grizzly Giant will still be standing and producing seeds a thousand years from now, in the year 3014.)

There was more Shenk wanted me to understand about giant sequoias. They're picky. They grow naturally only under certain conditions. A mature tree like the Grizzly Giant can have eleven thousand cones on its branches at a time (in some instances, forty thousand cones), most of them green and

closed, but on average two thousand of them turn brown each year and open to release their seeds. An average cone contains two hundred seeds, which means a single tree annually releases four hundred thousand seeds, each one with the same theoretical potential of becoming a giant tree living for three thousand years. Clearly it doesn't work out that way, otherwise the Mariposa Grove would have substantially more than the 481 adult trees counted in the most recent inventory, along with 736 juvenile trees, 1,500 saplings, and 3,000 seedlings. Only a very few seeds make that long journey to majestic maturity. But those that do, last through the ages.

As sequoias go, the Grizzly Giant is less graceful than most. On one side of its thick base, a blackened cavity rises fifteen feet or more to a sharp point—the deep scar from the many fires it has endured. The record encoded in tree rings of sequoias suggests that fires swept through the forests every five to ten years on average, either set by Indians or caused by lightning. In its two thousand years, the Grizzly Giant has been scorched hundreds of times. The fires were necessary to prepare the ground for the seeds to germinate, to eliminate the shade canopy of other tree species and create open spaces for the seedlings to grow into saplings, and to winnow out competitors as the surviving sapling matured into a thick-barked adult for whom a good blaze along the forest floor was at most an annoyance in the cycles of life.

Left: The Grizzly Giant, sketched in 1888

Opposite: The Mariposa Grove in 1911, with Galen Clark's cabin nestled in the center

The interruption of water and minerals up the Grizzly Giant's sapwood means its head has become a "snag-top"—not the rounded, broccoli-like crown of an unaltered sequoia (which are rare in old age), but jagged protrusions of dead wood left when pieces of the crown broke off over the centuries. The tree's massive branches extend without the slightest symmetry, rather in a haphazard way that suggests a multiarmed Goliath frozen in the moment he began to slip on a banana peel, with every appendage tossed akimbo. The sense of instability is heightened by the pronounced tilt of the tree's columnar trunk, leaning at a seventeen-degree angle into the slope. Within that angle hangs the possibility that this may be the moment the tree finally topples, bringing down twenty centuries of hard experience.

All of which, I think, gives this particular specimen more personality. Technically it may not be the oldest and biggest sequoia in existence, but the Grizzly Giant commands attention. It has unmistakable character, an aura of earned respect. If the majority of other trees in the Mariposa Grove seem like stately wooden sentinels in a silent temple of Nature, solemnly holding profound secrets, the Grizzly Giant comes across as equally sagacious, perhaps, but a little less cloistered and contemplative, more familiar with the rough and tumble of history, a seasoned veteran who has quite a few stories to tell if only it would share them.

◄○►

ONE HUNDRED AND FIFTY YEARS would comprise less than a tenth of the Grizzly Giant's life so far. That's more than a blink of an eye for something that measures time in centuries, but not much more. And yet, in that time, the giant sequoia has been intimately involved in more than its own incremental yet phenomenal growth. It has been connected to a shift in human history. A century and a half ago, the tree witnessed the birth of a new idea, watched that idea germinate like one of its own seeds, and personally met the people most responsible for the idea's development from seedling to sapling to something capable of producing its own seeds and regenerating its own species. That idea—that a nation's most majestic and sacred places should be preserved for everyone, and for all time—we now call the national park idea. At age 150, the national park idea seems such a natural part of our landscape that we often forget that it wasn't always so. We take it for granted that

the grandest canyon on earth or the nation's highest mountain or the world's greatest collection of geysers would of course be protected from destruction or despoliation. We assume that an exquisite valley with the continent's highest waterfalls and a grove of Creation's biggest trees would of course be saved for future generations to enjoy and experience. "Of course," we think, "that's only natural. That's the way it *should* be. That's the way it's *always* been." But in this last thought, we are mistaken.

Just like the Grizzly Giant, the national park idea was once just a seed.

Just like the Grizzly Giant, the national park idea was once just a seed—a seed encompassing the potential of something magnificent and monumental, but a seed that could just as easily have failed to take root and survive. There was nothing inevitable about it. Because history asks us to look backward, already knowing how things will end, we tend to ignore or overlook how uncertain the ending actually was at the beginning, or how many different endings were possible. Similarly, we can look at a sequoia tree and know that it came from a seed, even figure out its relationship to more ancient species of similar trees, but we can't know for sure that the seed on our fingertip will grow into a mature sequoia. History and biology and evolution are similar in that respect: better suited for discerning how things *became* what they are than for *predicting* what they will become.

National parks are simultaneously very real places and the embodiment of an idea, and that idea found its first home in a very real place. The place was the Yosemite Valley and Mariposa Grove of Giant Sequoias. From Yosemite the idea would spread to other places, evolving and changing as it grew and interacted with the world around it. Biology, ecology, evolution—and history, too—work that way: not just as mechanical processes of predictable cause and effect, but something more fluid, something that takes chance and choice and change into equal account, realizing the nearly infinite variables at play in the myriad interconnections of existence, and recognizing that the way things are now is not the *only* way things could have turned out.

Yosemite was not the world's first national park. Yellowstone holds that distinction. But Yellowstone National Park's creation came eight years after Yosemite was set aside by Congress and entrusted to the state of California. Its DNA was 99 percent that of Yosemite's, the only difference being which level of government was in charge. On an evolutionary tree, Yellowstone is a branch of Yosemite—a very big branch to be sure, like the one on the Grizzly Giant, but a branch nonetheless. So the best place to begin the story of the national park idea is at Yosemite, where it first sprouted, in 1864. The early years of Yosemite's experiment as a park, in the last half of the nineteenth century, took place when the nation

Opposite: Two women contemplate the ancient trees.

6

Above: During a respite from World War II, troops relax on the Fallen Monarch.

Opposite: Tourists in the 1880s demonstrate the girth of a giant sequoia.

was busily engaged in finishing its conquest of a continent. The principal business of Congress was disposing of the public domain by converting it to private property, and the prevailing attitude toward nature was encapsulated by how the Census Bureau described the westward-marching line it drew every ten years to mark the retreating frontier.

Once a place had a population density of more than two people per square mile, the Census Bureau said, it had been "redeemed from wilderness and brought into the service of man." Note this phrase: "redeemed *from* wilderness." A virgin forest, in other words, was "redeemed" when the trees were clear-cut. A wild-flowing river was "redeemed" by a dam. Miners could "redeem" mountainsides. Iron rails and

barbed wire could "redeem" the vast Plains. In retrospect, the act setting aside Yosemite Valley and the Mariposa Grove marked a dramatic break from this attitude, though at the time few people recognized it as such. It was seen as merely a slight, almost imperceptible deviation from the norm. But like so much in history—and evolution—a slight deviation can lead to more changes, and more still, leading in this case to a movement that would ultimately declare the exact opposite of what the Census Bureau had claimed: wilderness is not redeemed by man; man is redeemed by wilderness.

Besides being the birthplace of the national park idea, Yosemite provides the best case study of the idea's evolution, of the challenges that could have

stunted or even prevented growth of the movement, and especially of the basic types of human beings who have formed a symbiotic relationship with a place that became a national park. Every national park would eventually attract the same types of people, but here, too, Yosemite's champions were there first. While their DNA was not literally passed along to those who followed, they created archetypes that would be replicated in every subsequent interaction between Americans and their parks. Like Yosemite itself, each character was unique and yet representative of something larger. What a collection they are:

❡ James Mason Hutchings, a tireless promoter who first brought Yosemite to the world's attention; who loved the place nearly, but only nearly, as much as he loved the economic opportunity it offered him.

❡ Galen Clark, whose selfless devotion to Yosemite created the mold for those who commit themselves to caring for a special place not so much for financial gain but simply out of love of that place.

❡ Frederick Law Olmsted, whose response to Yosemite was aesthetic and intellectual, who became the first to express the democratic foundation of parks, and who, in looking toward a distant future, understood the need for regulations to preserve them.

❡ John Muir, the Prophet of the Wilderness, an "unknown nobody" who became the national voice of conservation, for whom the rationale for Yosemite and the national parks was not economic or democratic but deeply, viscerally spiritual.

Above: It was called the most photographed tree in the world—
and Galen Clark (holding the little girl's hand) was probably
Yosemite's most photographed person.

Opposite: The Wawona Tunnel Tree became one of Yosemite's
principal tourist attractions.

¶ And Theodore Roosevelt, who demonstrated what can happen when the spirit inherent in the idea first germinated in Yosemite finds a home in a person of action and political power.

Uniting all of them is how Yosemite influenced the trajectory of their individual lives, and in doing so influenced the trajectory of American history. All of them, it's worth noting, found some sort of redemption in Yosemite—spiritual, financial, physical, political, or personal—as if they were iron filings and Yosemite was the magnetic North that properly aligned them, pointing them in the direction that became their destiny. In that respect, they were redeemed by wilderness. In return, each played a part in preventing Yosemite from falling prey to the sad fate of so much of America's once pristine beauty; in doing so, they were redeeming Yosemite and helping it find a different destiny.

Also uniting all five men is the Grizzly Giant. Each of them spent time at the tree's thick-barked and gnarled feet, marveling at its size, pondering its age, confronting the same mind-challenging, soul-expanding questions of time and life that I was mulling a century and a half later, the questions posed by a speck of a seed and a colossus of a tree for whom the generations of humankind are almost too fleeting to bother counting. The Grizzly Giant had met us all—and innumerable others of our puny and comparatively short-lived species—and like a wise master, after planting the questions, left it to us to discover the answers.

◄○►

Park ranger Dean Shenk had some other places in the Mariposa Grove he wanted to show me. One was a small area where a controlled forest fire had been allowed to burn four years earlier. There, he and Monica Buhler, a restoration ecologist for the park, knelt down to point out things I would otherwise have overlooked: delicate little seedlings, maybe five inches tall, supple and fragile. They had sprouted in the fire's immediate aftermath, the most ideal condition for new sequoias to get started, when the normal layer of duff has burned off to expose bare soil, and when a pocket of light has been created by eliminating the mantle of shade from other tree species and bushes. In that spot of open soil and open sunlight, the seeds have their best shot at regenerating the species.

Ironically, for most of the past 150 years, since humans undertook to protect the ancient sequoias by vigilantly suppressing fires in the groves, sequoia reproduction essentially stopped. Galen Clark, credited with being the first white man to see the grove and who dedicated his life to preserving it, worked tirelessly at putting out fires whenever he could, all for the sake of his beloved trees. He and other sequoia protectors like John Muir duly noted the increase in the number of seedlings after a fire, but the conservation ethic they were developing had not yet connected the dots. Muir's studies of glaciers and

Opposite: Three men in 1908 are dwarfed by the sequoias' majestic trunks.

their role in reshaping landscapes had revealed to him that "Nature is ever at work building and pulling down, creating and destroying," but he couldn't quite bring himself to see a forest fire the same way. So the cardinal rule at the time was to extinguish all fires as quickly and thoroughly as possible. The result was a double whammy: fewer sequoia seeds germinated for lack of proper conditions, and those fires that did get going could sometimes be catastrophically destructive because of the accumulation of undergrowth and deadfall in the absence of more regular, smaller fires.

Eventually scientists persuaded park managers to change policies. Some naturally occurring fires are now allowed to run their course; in other instances, controlled burns are conducted. Shenk took me to a spot, near the famous Telescope Tree, where one of the first controlled burns occurred, in 1971. "Our kindergarten group," he called it, the first class of new sequoias in about a century and a half. They formed a cluster of thin trees about thirty feet high and eight inches in diameter. One of them may ultimately reach the age and size of the Grizzly Giant and its elders. Standing in their collective presence I was in touch with living things that were already two thousand to three thousand years old and their children, who would be alive and standing two thousand to three thousand years from now—a span of time stretching nearly *six thousand years*. Such a moment rearranges your notion of "generations from now."

There was a lesson the sequoias were trying to teach me.

From the ancient sequoias' perspective, the 150 years of fire suppression was a mistake but ultimately just a momentary interruption in their self-propagation. The lesson the trees have taught us with their patience is that our efforts at preservation can backfire. Our good intentions had saved the Mariposa Grove from being cut down by loggers but, for a while, threatened to snuff out a succeeding generation of trees. Good intentions are essential in the creation of any national park, but never enough. Over the long haul, caring for a national park takes a willingness to learn and adapt: we make mistakes and then we make adjustments.

For me, someone more conversant in the workings of history than environmental science, there was a lesson the sequoias were trying to teach me. For something as unique as the national park idea to be born, it required a certain combination of conditions; for the idea to survive and succeed, it needed to evolve, while keeping most of its DNA intact. If I wanted to understand the birth and evolution of the national park idea, Yosemite and the Mariposa Grove was the place to start. My understanding would be deepened if I paused to give more thought to the life of a sequoia, from seed to seedling to sapling to Grizzly Giant—if I considered history as a process more like biology than physics or mathematics, not an orderly progression of events or an equation of additions and subtractions but an evolution much more

organic and unruly and unpredictable. I needed to think like a sequoia.

The early years are the riskiest. For even a tiny fraction of a sequoia's seeds to germinate, the soil must be just right—often the result, tree specialists have written, "after the environment experiences a disturbance." The odds against a seedling then surviving to sapling stage and of a sapling becoming an adult are equally steep. I decided to concentrate first on the germination stage of the national park idea, when two of the nation's greatest "disturbances" occurred (the Gold Rush and the Civil War) and the seed was planted and, ultimately, when it sprouted. Then I needed to examine the early years of the idea, its most vulnerable stage, when its growth was still uncertain and its very existence was in greatest peril, when it needed individual people to nourish it until it could be well rooted enough to become strong and tall and majestic. I bid farewell to the Grizzly Giant. The historical story I was pursuing—and the people animating it—would bring me back.

I

THE
TESTIMONY
OF THE
ROCKS

Long ago, two little bear cubs living in the Valley of Ah-wah-nee went down to the river to swim. They paddled and splashed about to their hearts' content. The cubs then returned to shore and climbed up on a huge boulder that stood beside the water. They lay down to dry themselves in the warm sunshine, and very soon they fell asleep.

Meanwhile, the great rock upon which they slept began to rise. It rose day and night, little by little, until it had lifted them up high into the sky. In this way the cubs were carried out of sight and beyond voice of their bird and animal friends below.

They were lifted up into the blue heavens, far up, far up, until the little bears scraped their faces against the moon. Still they slumbered and slept year after year, safe among the clouds.

—THE LEGEND OF TU-TOK-A-NU'-LA

IN WHAT HAS OFTEN BEEN called the "discovery" of Yosemite Valley, in the early spring of 1851 a group of fifty-eight white men from the Mariposa Battalion were traveling through heavy snow and dense trees, on their way from what is now Wawona, when they suddenly emerged from the woods and found themselves on the elevated perch of what came to be known as Inspiration Point. It was late afternoon, and the lowering sun cast long shadows across the immense cliff faces framing the dramatic view up the Valley's mouth. One of the privates, a twenty-seven-year-old Mexican War veteran from Michigan named Lafayette Houghton Bunnell, lingered to gaze in wonder at the sight. Like so many who would follow, Bunnell considered the vista before him—and the emotions it evoked—so overwhelming that it was "utterly indescribable." But then he felt compelled to try:

> The grandeur of the scene was but softened by the haze that hung over the valley—light as gossamer—and by the clouds which partially dimmed the higher cliffs and mountains. This obscurity of vision but increased the awe with which I beheld it, and as I looked, a peculiar exalted sensation seemed to fill my whole being, and I found my eyes in tears with emotion.
>
> I said with some enthusiasm, . . . "I have here seen the power and glory of a Supreme being; the majesty of His handy-work is in that 'Testimony of the Rocks.'"

With that, the Mariposa Battalion entered the Valley and Yosemite officially entered the historical record. But like all of history, the truth is consid-

Dr. Lafayette Bunnell

erably messier and more complicated. As with so many things related to Yosemite, the story of its "discovery" neatly distills and encapsulates the broader brush of American history, in this case the treatment (and even recognition) of native peoples. The Mariposa Battalion no more "discovered" Yosemite Valley than Columbus had "discovered" the New World; though, like Columbus, it did bring a place to the attention of the rest of the world and did give it the name that stuck. (Intent on finding a new route to "the regions of India," Columbus called the islands he encountered in the Caribbean the "Indies" and their inhabitants the "Indios" or Indians. More than

five hundred years later, we're still captives of his miscalculation.)

Like Lewis and Clark, who did not blaze a path across an unpopulated West but instead often followed well-worn trails and relied on guidance from the dozens of tribes they met along the way, the Mariposa Battalion not only took an old Indian trail from Wawona, but on their way to the Valley that morning they also met a group of seventy-two Indians coming *out* of it. So the remote Sierra Nevada valley Bunnell and his companions "discovered" hardly qualified as

part of the Unknown. It was already well known by somebody. It was, in fact, their home and had been for a very long time. By 1851 the members of the Mariposa Battalion could actually be considered latecomers, but because theirs was the first account reported back to the non-native world, to them goes the distinction of what is often called *effective discovery*.

Even here, history is messy. In 1833 the mountain man Joseph Walker had led a group of sixty trappers across the Sierra Nevada somewhere along the divide between the Merced and Tuolumne Rivers.

They most certainly saw the Merced or Tuolumne grove of giant sequoias (and possibly both), and they may or may not have looked down into Yosemite Valley. (A one-paragraph description by Zenas Leonard, the only chronicler of their adventure, is both vague and remarkably unexcited.) But once the Valley became famous, Walker liked to claim that he was the first white man to see it, and he asked that his tombstone proclaim this as fact. In 1849 a carpenter named William Penn Abrams and his friend U. N. Reamer were hunting a grizzly bear when they followed its tracks into a valley Abrams described in his diary as "enclosed by stupendous cliffs rising perhaps 3,000 feet" and "a waterfall [that] dropped from a cliff below three jagged peaks . . . while farther beyond, a rounded mountain stood, the valley side of which looked as though it had been sliced with a knife as one would slice a loaf of bread, and which Reamer and I called the Rock of Ages." These are clearly descriptions of Cathedral Rocks, Bridalveil Fall, and Half Dome, but unfortunately for Abrams's place in history, his diary entry was itself not "discovered" until 1947, nearly a century later. Call it *ineffective discovery*, but without a doubt, Abrams was there two years before Bunnell and felt something of the same religious stirrings—enough, at least, to quote a popular hymn ("Rock of Ages, cleft for me. . . .") when surrounded by the granite walls.

Opposite: The timeless view up the mouth of Yosemite Valley, with El Capitan on the left, Half Dome peeking up in the distant center, and Bridalveil Fall on the right

⌐◦¬

THE PEOPLE WHO CONSIDERED the Valley home—the ones Bunnell met as the Mariposa Battalion was on its way to "discovery"—called it Ah-wah-nee, the place of the gaping mouth. To show their complete identification with the Valley, they called themselves the Ahwahneechees. Descendants of Indians who had first begun inhabiting the Valley roughly seven thousand years earlier, they had, over time, attached their own names to the prominent landmarks around them. Cho'-lok (Yosemite Falls, the highest waterfall in North America) and Po-ho'-no (Bridalveil Fall), each with its own spirits, brought them fresh water from the high country. The massive Tu-tok-a-nu'-la (El Capitan, the largest granite monolith in the world) derived its name from the legend of the only living thing said to have climbed its sheer cliff and saved two bear cubs stranded at its top, when every other animal had failed: a lowly measuring worm that made the vertical three-thousand-foot ascent an inch at a time.

Half Dome was not the Rock of Ages. It was Tis-se'-yak, in memory of a woman near the beginnings of time who, according to legend, came to the Valley with a large basket of acorns on her back and stopped to drink from A-wai'-a (Mirror Lake). She was so thirsty, the story went, that she drank all the lake's water, angering her husband, who had lagged behind and arrived thirsty himself. When he began beating Tis-se'-yak with his staff, she threw her basket of acorns at him in retaliation. For breaking the peace of the Valley, the quarrelsome

couple was instantly turned to stone, condemned to stare at each other throughout eternity: North Dome (or sometimes Washington Column) is the husband, Basket Dome is the discarded basket, and most distinctive of all is Tis-se'-yak, whose flat face still exhibits the dark stains of her tears. Long before Yosemite's granite inspired both Bunnell and Abrams, those rocks were testifying to the human beings gathered at their feet.

Within the sheltered valley, over the centuries the Ahwahneechees established more than thirty different village sites, occupied at one time or another. The people lived in *u-ma-chas*, conical structures framed with poles and covered with long slabs of incense cedar bark—remarkably watertight in bad weather and relatively warm during winters when filled with a family crowded around a fire in the center. They survived on the deer they killed, the fish they caught, and particularly the acorns they gathered from the abundant black oak trees on the Valley floor. The acorns were pounded against the rock mortar basins the people chiseled into the granite bedrock. When they had produced a fine yellow meal, the people leached it of its tannins by repeated soakings and finally cooked it into acorn mush. This was hard, time-consuming work, but the Valley provided what the Ahwahneechees needed to survive. In preparation for winter, they dried strips of meat and stored acorns—up to one hundred pounds, a year's worth for a family—in granaries called *chuck-ahs* that were covered with tightly interwoven deer brush and grapevine and lined with aromatic wormwood

to repel insects and rodents. Rather than making pottery, they wove intricate baskets from the abundant variety of plants around them, crafting different designs and sizes to hold everything from water to acorn mush, from babies to heavy burdens.

Like native peoples across the continent at the time, the Ahwahneechees lived more lightly on the land than those who would follow them, but they were hardly passive inhabitants of the environment. They tried to alter it for their own purposes. If it helped in harvesting acorns, they broke off the lower branches of the black oaks. If the water was low in the Merced River and its tributary streams, they stopped using spears and weirs to catch rainbow trout and instead created a mixture of pulverized soaproot to make the water foamy, suffocating the fish, which rose to the surface for easy collection. And on a regular basis, they set fire to the Valley floor, burning off the young pines and cedars that would otherwise crowd out the precious black oaks, and encouraging new growth of grasses that attracted the deer as browse.

Isolated as Ah-wah-nee seemed to Bunnell and the Mariposa Battalion, it was not cut off from the rest of the native world. The Ahwahneechees fought, traded, and sometimes intermarried with neighboring tribes, especially the Miwoks in the foothills and lowlands to the west and the Mono Paiutes in the deserts over the crest of the Sierra. The Miwoks and Paiutes, in turn, did the same with their neighbors—part of a web of trading and interaction that connected all American Indians across the conti-

A Miwok girl and woman outside their cedar-bark *u-ma-cha*
in Yosemite Valley, 1887

nent more intimately than is commonly understood. Ahwahneechee women who had never seen the ocean used seashells for decoration; Ahwahneechee men who had never crossed the mountains relied on glassy chunks of obsidian from Mono Lake volcanic craters for their arrow points and hide scrapers. And sometime near the end of the 1700s, although they had never encountered white people, nearly all of the Ahwahneechees perished from a white man's disease (probably smallpox or cholera) that had traveled the same trade routes from the coast—just one of the many European diseases that pulsed throughout North America for three-hundred-plus years after Columbus. These diseases laid waste to people who had no natural immunities against them, creating far more unintentional devastation in terms of body count than any of the deliberate cruelties that often followed the first contacts.

For the Ahwahneechees, the "fatal black sickness" left so few survivors that they abandoned their beloved Valley to seek refuge with their neighbors. During this diaspora, one of the chiefs married a Mono Paiute woman, who gave birth to a son named Tenaya. The boy grew up in the eastern desert listening to tales of the grassy Valley on the other side of the mountains, and around 1820, perhaps at the advice of an Ahwahneechee medicine man, he decided to return and reclaim the land for his father's people. Tenaya's band totaled around two hundred people: some of them Ahwahneechee descendants, but also refugees and outcasts from other tribes in the region. Back in the "place of the gaping mouth,"

they prospered once more. Tenaya grew older and watched his children have children of their own. Then disaster struck again.

◄◦►

OF ALL THE SAD REFRAINS that constitute the story of Indian-white relations in American history, none is sadder than the one that begins: "And then gold was discovered on their land. . . ." From the Cherokees in Georgia to the Lakotas in the Black Hills to the Nez Percé in Idaho, once that sentence found utterance, things inevitably ended badly for the original inhabitants. For California's native peoples, the tragedy assumed staggering proportions. By 1848 an estimated 150,000 Indians lived in California—itself a figure cut in half in the century since the first Spanish priests came north from Mexico and established missions where coastal tribes were forced to work and convert to Christianity. Because of disease, poor food, poor treatment, and in some cases simple despair, Indian populations within the coastal strip of missions stretching from San Diego to San Francisco had dropped from seventy-two thousand to as few as eighteen thousand. "They live well free," one friar observed, "but as soon as we reduce them to a Christian and community life . . . they fatten, sicken and die." As the Ahwahneechees had learned, the reach of the white man's diseases extended far beyond the missions. If 300,000 Indians populated California in precontact times, they numbered 50 percent fewer just before the area became part of the United States.

The California Gold Rush attracted swarms of newcomers, rearranging the streams and spelling doom for the native people.

When the news of gold at Sutter's Mill, and of fabulous riches littering the streams of the western Sierra foothills, reverberated across the world in 1848, it touched off an unprecedented onslaught of newcomers. Tens of thousands swarmed the riverbanks, stripping the mining regions of fish and game to feed themselves. In their frenzy for gold, they diverted water to expedite the search, so that a typical tributary, one miner wrote, became "so thick with mud that it will scarcely run." With their natural supplies of sustenance dwindling, some Indians hired themselves out to pan for gold in exchange for the white man's food and clothing. Many of the miners resented the competition. The new state of California outlawed slavery, but it permitted any jobless Indian to be declared a vagrant and have his or her services auctioned off for up to four months. Another law allowed whites to force Indian children to work for them, provided they got permission from a parent or "friend." The resulting abuses included raids to kidnap Indian children from their villages to be sold as "apprentices" for a hundred dollars. Further greasing the system, yet another law said that no Indian (or black or mulatto) could provide evidence against a white person.

Not surprisingly, some Indians resisted the invasion. They stole horses and cattle, raided small mining camps, fought back. The result was an even greater retaliation against *all* Indians. The towns of Marysville and Honey Lake paid bounties for Indian scalps, while Shasta City offered five dollars for every

CALIFORNIA GOLD DIGGERS.
Mining Operations on the Western shore of the Sacramento River

A lithograph shows the mixed population at the diggings in the front, while a fight breaks out in the right rear.

Indian head brought to city hall. In the Pitt River valley a contingent of volunteers fell upon an Indian village, killing nine men before the other warriors escaped. Forty women and children surrendered, thinking they would be spared. They weren't. "The miners . . . are sometimes guilty of the most brutal acts," a forty-niner named William Swain wrote his wife. "Such incidents have fallen under my notices that would make humanity weep and men disown their race." In what became the worst sustained slaughter of native people in American history, during the twenty years following the Gold Rush the number of Indians in California fell from 150,000 to fewer than 30,000.

The federal government made earnest, though ultimately ineffective, efforts to stem the brutal chaos by trying to establish reservations where the Indians could be simultaneously protected and out of the way of the main business, which was mining. (California's delegation to Congress would eventually block ratification of the treaties the federal agents negotiated.) Part of that effort gave birth to the Mariposa Battalion, under the command of James D. Savage. He had arrived in California in 1846, worked briefly for John Sutter, and by 1851 had established extensive relations with the Yokuts (he married several Yokut women), Chowchillas, and other tribes near his trading posts on the Fresno River and Mariposa Creek.

In the bloody context of his time and place, Savage might be considered more humane in his treatment of the natives: he employed many of them in the gold diggings and seemingly paid them fairly for their efforts, and he took the Yokuts' side when they complained that the treaty he had helped negotiate was being brazenly ignored by white miners. Still, when Savage and his men arrived in Yosemite Valley on March 27, 1851, there was no question in his mind about his mission: he was there to drive out the Indians who lived there, one way or another, and force them onto a reservation.

Savage had already met Tenaya during the Mariposa Battalion's encampment at Wawona. The aging chief told him what many other Indian leaders would tell military leaders across the West at similar moments for the rest of the century. He did not want war but could not convince everyone in his tribe that peace on the white man's terms was a better alternative:

I have talked with my people and told them I was going to see the white chiefs sent to make peace. I was told I was growing old, and it was well that I should go, but that young and strong men can find plenty in the mountains; therefore why should they go [to the reservation], to be yarded like horses and cattle. My heart has been sore since that talk, but I am now willing to go, for it is best for my people that I do so.

Major Savage's response to Tenaya's poignant speech, Bunnell later wrote, was "Forward march!" He sent the old chief, with the seventy-two others they had met, back to the expedition's main force at Wawona and moved toward the Valley. At Inspiration Point, when Bunnell stopped in rapture at the scene, Savage broke the reverie by calling out,

Bridalveil Fall, which the Ahwahneechees called Po-ho'-no

"Wake up from that dream." He pushed his troops forward. Just as Tenaya had predicted, they found no Indians in the Valley except an old woman too frail to flee; the others had all escaped up the canyons toward the high country. But the battalion did find the Ahwahneechees' cedar-bark *u-ma-chas* filled with the Indians' belongings and their *chuck-ahs* crammed with acorns (nearly six hundred bushels, Bunnell estimated). Just as Kit Carson would do thirteen years later in Canyon de Chelly on his mission to subjugate the Navajos, Savage ordered everything burned—the huts, the finely woven baskets, the stores of food.

With the Valley hazed by smoke from all the fires, the battalion encamped near Bridalveil Fall. Still in the thrall of the grandeur around him, Bunnell suggested that they give the Valley a proper name. "An American name would be most appropriate," he said. "I then proposed that we give the valley the name of Yo-sem-i-ty, as it was suggestive, euphonious, and certainly *American*; that by so doing the name of the tribe of Indians which we met leaving their homes in this valley, perhaps never to return, would be perpetuated." The interpreters for the Mariposa Battalion were mission Indians, Bunnell reported, and the way they and Major Savage understood what the Valley's tribe was called came out through a thicket of possible misinterpretations. It boiled down to a version of "Yo-sem-i-ty" or "O-soom-i-ty" or "Uzamati" and was thought to signify grizzly bears.

Others wanted names taken from Scripture or suggestive of foreign landmarks. A man named

Tunnehill, dead set against an Indian name ("Why should we honor these vagabond murderers by perpetuating their names!" he explained) nominated "Paradise Valley," which for a brief moment seemed to gather support. But on a voice vote, Bunnell's laudatory impulse to at least honor the original inhabitants prevailed. "Yosemite" it became.

Here, too, history was repeating and echoing itself. On their way west in 1804, Lewis and Clark had met a tribe in the Bitterroot Valley of what is now Montana. Relying on information neighboring tribes had provided, and possibly misinterpreting sign language, they called the people Flatheads, although this particular group did not practice flattening the heads of their infants, as people along the Columbia River did. The tribe referred to themselves as the Salish, but since the moment they met the Corps of Discovery, the people of the Bitterroot have had to contend with being termed Flatheads. Likewise, the Lakotas of the Plains were never the Sioux, except in the language of their enemies the Ojibwe, who used the term—roughly meaning "snake in the grass"—when they told French explorers about the people over the next horizon. Thus the Lakotas became the tribe named Sioux. Being conquered and dispossessed is bad enough. Having to live with a different name, particularly a derogatory one, is an additional insult. If the flow of history and conquest had been reversed, and Native American explorers had asked the English for the name of the Teutonic people farther east, we might now officially call the Germans "krauts" and expect them to live with it.

In the case of the Ahwahneechees, Bunnell, it should be remembered, was acting out of commendable motives. He didn't want the original inhabitants to be forgotten. He identified them honorably as "Americans." And but for his persistence, posterity would have been stuck with one of the continent's most awe-inspiring and unique landscapes being forever known as Paradise Valley, something a not very imaginative real-estate agent might come up with. Nonetheless, the name was a mistake: The closest thing to "Yosemite" in the Ahwahneechee dialect is probably a corruption of "Yo-che-ma-te." It means "some of them are killers."

FOR TENAYA AND HIS PEOPLE, the aftermath of Yosemite's "discovery" brought more heartache. A second Mariposa Battalion expedition in May 1851 finally managed to capture the remaining Ahwahneechees at the lake that now bears Tenaya's name. The chief's youngest son was shot in the back by a soldier who seemed happy to have killed an Indian. The tribe was moved to the Fresno River reservation, where the lowland climate, government food, and hostility of other tribes confined in the same space made life miserable. Promising not to create trouble with the whites, Tenaya was allowed to return home and was soon joined by more Ahwahneechees. But in 1852, when eight prospectors entered the Valley and two were killed, the regular army was dispatched. The soldiers caught six Indians and promptly executed them, then pursued Tenaya and his band all the way

east over the mountains to Mono Lake but failed to catch them. In the summer of 1853, Tenaya returned again to the Valley, but some of his young men stole a string of horses from their former hosts, the Monos, provoking the Paiutes to seek revenge and resulting in Tenaya being stoned to death in the attack.

Once more, the Ahwahneechees dispersed among other tribes, and this time they never fully regrouped as a distinct people. Over the years a few returned to the Valley and established tiny communities in the early 1900s, finding work from white settlers or selling baskets to tourists, the remnants of a people dispossessed by a man named Savage from a home whose very name had been taken away.

The most famous reunion of Ahwahneechee and the Valley they knew as Ah-wah-nee occurred in the summer of 1929. A ninety-year-old woman called Maria Lebrado showed up. She was the granddaughter of Tenaya, who would have known her as Totuya ("Foaming Water"). Seventy-eight years earlier, not quite a teenager, she had been among the group of Ahwahneechees that Savage and Bunnell and the Mariposa Battalion encountered struggling out of the Valley back in 1851. She represented the last living survivor of that sad moment in her people's history.

Above: Tenaya Lake, named for the chief of the Ahwahneechees

Opposite: Suzie and Sadie McGowen, Mono Lake Paiutes, with Yosemite Falls in the background, around 1900

Totuya, the granddaughter of Tenaya and last survivor of the
Mariposa Battalion's incursion of 1851, describes her people's
travails to George Melendez Wright in 1929.

In the intervening years, Totuya had married, become a mother, and settled near the town of Mariposa, steadfastly refusing to return to her old home. Too many bitter memories. But that summer, the black oaks' acorns were particularly abundant and she arrived to gather her share, living in a tent with one of her daughters in the Indian village behind the park museum, pounding her harvest with a stone pestle, leeching it of its tannin, and cooking acorn mush as her people always had. Word of her presence reached park officials, who wanted desperately to hear her stories. George Melendez Wright, a young biologist on the staff, and others reached out to her. Wright especially endeared himself to her with his friendly charm and his ability to speak to her in Spanish.

They took her to the small cemetery nearby, where one of her cousins was buried. The gravesite brought Totuya to the realization that she was the only person left who had lived in the Valley before the white man's arrival. "All gone, long, long time 'go," she said sadly in a mixture of Spanish, English, and her native tongue. "I 'lone." In the museum's Indian Room her eyes brightened to see the exhibits. She strapped on a baby cradle and walked around happily, saying "Papoose, long time 'go." She fondled the obsidian arrowheads with her gnarled hands and recalled her people's annual gatherings with the Monos to trade their acorns for the shiny stone. She went through the display of baskets, identifying from each one's design which tribe had made it and critically judging its quality.

Then they took Totuya outside to tour the place she once knew so intimately. The meadows had become overgrown with saplings and bushes. "Too dirty," she scolded, "too much bushy." In her day the Ahwahneechees' regular fires would not have permitted this. The names of all the Valley's familiar features had been changed, but she recognized them, one witness recounted, as if she had never gone away. She saluted the great stone monolith of Tu-tok-a-nu'-la. (On the belief that the natives called it "Chief Rock," and trying to please his Spanish-speaking interpreters from the missions, Bunnell had given it the name of El Capitan.) Totuya turned to Loya (Sentinel Rock), which had loomed over her childhood home, and after a brief silence, spoke to it: "Loya, Loya; long time 'go." Yosemite Falls still poured over the cliffs as they always had, and she greeted them too, as if, one witness recounted, the rushing waters "spoke to her as they had spoken in her childhood." Totuya gave a happy answer: "Cho'-lok! Cho'-lok no gone!" Then, turning toward Half Dome, the cleft rock she still knew as Tis-se'-yak, she stretched out her arms and raised her voice in a strong, clear, high-pitched call—the same call, she explained, that her grandfather Tenaya had once used to summon his people together. The voice echoing back, fainter but distinct, was the testimony of the rocks.

If you can look into the seeds of time,

And say which grain will grow and which will not,

Speak, then, to me. . . .

—MACBETH, ACT 1, SCENE 3

CONTENTS

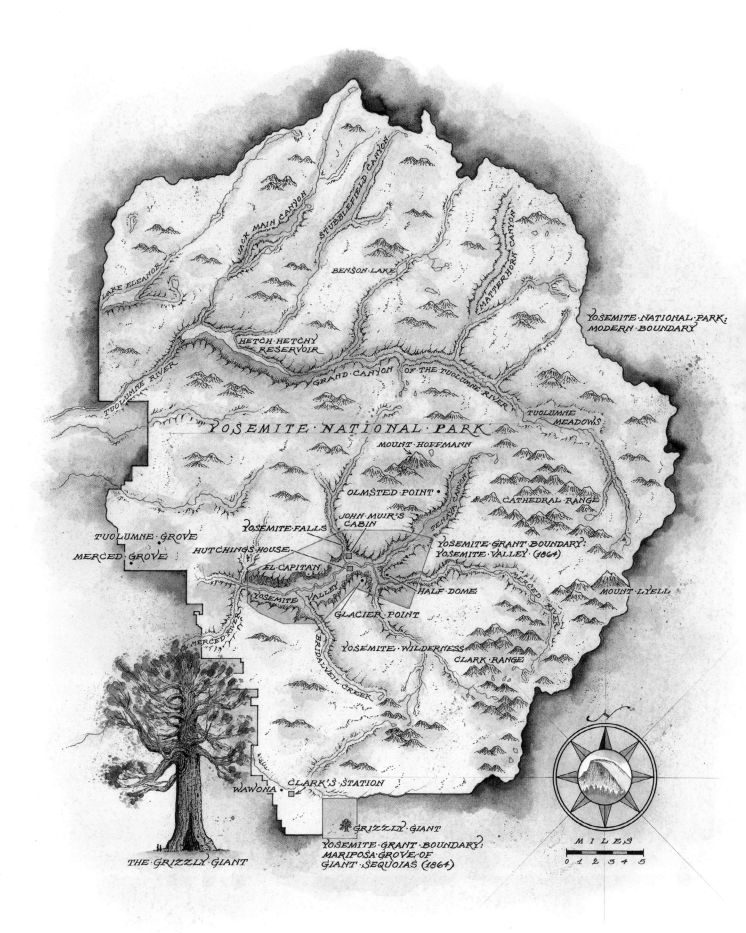

YOSEMITE·NATIONAL·PARK: MODERN·BOUNDARY

JACK·MAIN·CANYON

STUBBLEFIELD·CANYON

MATTERHORN·CANYON

LAKE·ELEANOR

BENSON·LAKE

HETCH·HETCHY RESERVOIR

TUOLUMNE·RIVER

GRAND·CANYON·OF·THE·TUOLUMNE·RIVER

TUOLUMNE MEADOWS

YOSEMITE · NATIONAL · PARK

MOUNT·HOFFMANN

OLMSTED·POINT·

CATHEDRAL·RANGE

TENAYA·CANYON

YOSEMITE·FALLS

JOHN·MUIR'S CABIN

TUOLUMNE·GROVE

HUTCHINGS·HOUSE

YOSEMITE·GRANT·BOUNDARY: YOSEMITE·VALLEY·(1864)

MERCED·GROVE

EL·CAPITAN

MERCED·RIVER

HALF·DOME·

YOSEMITE·VALLEY

MOUNT·LYELL

GLACIER·POINT

MERCED·RIVER

YOSEMITE·WILDERNESS

CLARK·RANGE

BRIDALVEIL·CREEK

CLARK'S·STATION

WAWONA

GRIZZLY·GIANT

THE·GRIZZLY·GIANT

YOSEMITE·GRANT·BOUNDARY: MARIPOSA·GROVE·OF GIANT·SEQUOIAS·(1864)

MILES

0 1 2 3 4 5

Yosemite Park is a place of rest, a refuge from the roar and dust and weary, nervous, wasting work of the lowlands, in which one gains the advantages of both solitude and society.

This one noble park is big enough and rich enough for a whole life of study and aesthetic enjoyment. It is good for everybody, no matter how benumbed with care, encrusted with a mail of business habits like a tree with bark. None can escape its charms. Its natural beauty cleanses and warms like fire, and you will be willing to stay in one place like a tree.

—JOHN MUIR

THIS BOOK IS DEDICATED to anyone—past, present,

or future—who not only loves Yosemite, but also cherishes it enough to

nourish and protect it. As John Muir himself would say, "The trees and

their lovers will sing [your] praises, and generations yet unborn will rise up

and call [you] blessed."

─◄◦►─

YOSEMITE
CONSERVANCY.

yosemiteconservancy.org

Through the support of donors, Yosemite Conservancy provides grants and support
to Yosemite National Park to help preserve and protect Yosemite today and for
future generations. The work funded by Yosemite Conservancy is visible throughout
the park, from trail rehabilitation to wildlife protection and habitat restoration.
The Conservancy is dedicated to enhancing the visitor experience and providing a
deeper connection to the park through outdoor programs, volunteering and wilderness services. Thanks to dedicated supporters, the Conservancy has provided more
than $80 million in grants to Yosemite National Park.

Library of Congress Control Number: 2013938232

Cover photograph by Matthew Crowley / Matthew Crowley Photography
Cover design by Nancy Austin
Interior design by Nancy Austin

Manufactured using recycled paper and soy inks.
All materials are from sustainable sources.

FSC
www.fsc.org
MIX
Paper from
responsible sources
FSC® C002589

Hardcover ISBN 978-1-930238-41-1 / Paperback ISBN 978-1-930238-42-8

Printed in the United States of America by Worzalla

1 2 3 4 5 6 – 17 16 15 14 13

SEED
of the
FUTURE

YOSEMITE AND THE EVOLUTION
OF THE NATIONAL PARK IDEA

Dayton Duncan

YOSEMITE CONSERVANCY
Yosemite National Park

2
AS FAMED
AS
NIAGARA

The first view of this convulsion-rent valley, with its perpendicular mountain cliffs, deep gorges, and awful chasms, spread out before us like a mysterious scroll, took away the power of thinking, much less clothing thoughts with suitable language.

When the inexpressible first impression had been overcome and human tongues had regained the power of speech, such exclamations as the following were uttered—"Oh! Now let me die, for I am happy."

—JAMES MASON HUTCHINGS

A VALLEY AS SPECTACULAR AS YOSEMITE is hard to keep secret. But given the times and the circumstances of its "discovery," word of its grandeur at first leaked out more than it gushed. "We were not a party of tourists," Lafayette Bunnell had conceded in 1851 about the Mariposa Battalion. "Our business there was to find Indians who were endeavoring to escape." What few reports of the battalion's activities reached San Francisco newspapers dealt mostly with the removal of the Indians, prompting a few groups of miners and hunters (including James

Capen "Grizzly" Adams) to deem it safe enough to visit the Valley in 1853 and 1854. In all, maybe a few more than a dozen visited, but no more. One newspaper account, however, mentioned a waterfall "nearly a thousand feet high"—six times the height of Niagara's. That nugget of information caught the restless and ambitious eye of someone who was prospecting for a different kind of gold, and in turn changed Yosemite's history forever.

By 1855, James Mason Hutchings had long since decided that the hard work of mining was not

James Mason Hutchings

his path to riches or glory. An Englishman by birth, he had abandoned his father's trade of carpentry after an exhibit in Birmingham of the American artist George Catlin's western scenes fired his imagination to emigrate. Following a brief stint writing for the New Orleans *Daily Picayune*, Hutchings joined the rush to California in 1849 and did well enough in the diggings near Placerville to deposit his earnings for purchase of San Francisco house lots. But the real-estate company folded and took his money down with it. He went back to mining, accumulated sixty thousand dollars to invest in a water-ditch and canal company, and then saw that evaporate as well.

Hutchings regrouped again, only to have a bank collapse and erase his gains once more. "Such is change in California," he said, and started over, again.

Like so many other entrepreneurs drawn to California in that first tectonic boom, Hutchings had a knack for shaking off failure. His attention always focused on the next big chance. He found it by publishing "The Miner's Ten Commandments," an illustrated letter sheet spoofing the original biblical commandments ("Thou shalt not grow discouraged, nor think of going home before thou hast made thy 'pile,'" and so on) that he sold for up to fifty cents each, traveling from one mining district to another. Nearly one hundred thousand copies were snapped up. Hutchings followed it with other publishing successes: "Commandments to California Wives," lithographs and descriptions of the Calaveras big trees, and stereographic daguerreotypes of mining towns that lonely prospectors could send home to their loved ones (or take with them when they went bust and headed home in person).

For a promoter like Hutchings, the prospect of publicizing a thousand-foot waterfall tucked away in a recess of the Sierra proved irresistible. In July of 1855 he set off from San Francisco, only to learn in the town of Mariposa that no one there, including some veterans of Savage's battalion, seemed to know how to find the place he wanted so keenly to see with his own eyes. Finally, after hiring two members of Tenaya's band as guides and enduring three days of rough going through thick underbrush, he and three companions arrived at Inspiration Point,

No. I.

No. II.

No. III.

No. VII.

No. VIII.

No. IX.

THE MINER'S TEN COMMANDMENTS.

A man spake these words and said: I am a miner, who wandered "from away down east," and came to sojourn in a strange land and "see the elephant." And behold I saw him, and bear witness, that from the key of his trunk to the end of his tail, his whole body has passed before me; and I followed him until his huge feet stood still before a clapboard shanty; then, with his trunk extended, he pointed to a candle-card tacked upon a shingle, and I read the

Miners' Ten Commandments.

I.

Thou shalt have no other claim than one.

II.

Thou shalt not make unto thyself any false claim, nor any likeness to a mean man, by jumping one; whatever thou findest on the top above, or on the rock beneath, or in a crevice underneath the rock — or I will visit the miners around to invite them on thy side; and when they decide against thee, thou shalt take thy pick and thy pan, thy shovel, and thy blankets, with all that thou hast, and "go prospect ing," to seek good diggings; but thou shalt find none. Then, when thou hast returned, in sorrow shalt thou find that thine old claim is worked out, and yet no pile made thee, to hide in the ground, or in an old boot beneath thy bunk, or in buckskin or bottle underneath thy dirty cabin; but hast paid all that was in thy purse away, worn out thy boots and thy garments, so that there is nothing gained but that there pockets, and thy patience is likened unto thy garments; and at last thou shalt hire thy body out to make thy board and save thy bacon.

III.

Thou shalt not go prospecting before thy claim gives out. Neither shalt thou take thy money, nor thy gold dust, nor thy good name, to the gaming table in vain; for monte, twenty-one, roulette, faro, lansquenet and poker, will prove to thee that the more thou put test down the less thou shalt take up; and when thou thinkest of thy wife and children, thou shalt not hold thyself guiltless, but—insane.

IV.

Thou shalt not remember what thy friends do at home on the Sabbath day, lest the remembrance may not compare favorably with what thou doest here. Six days thou mayest dig or pick all that thy body can stand under; but the other day is Sunday; yet thou washest all thy dirty shirts, darnest all thy stockings, tap thy boots, mend thy clothing, chop thy whole week's firewood, make up and bake thy bread and boil thy pork and beans, that thou wait not when thou returnest from thy long-tom, weary. For in six days' labor only thou canst not work enough to wear out thy body in two years; but if thou workest hard on Sunday also, thou canst do it in six months; and thou, and thy son, and thy daughter, thy male friend and thy female friend, thy morals and thy conscience, be none the better for it; but reproach thee, shouldst thou ever return with thy worn-out body to thy mother's fireside; and thou strive to justify thyself, because the trader and the blacksmith, the carpenter and the merchant, the sailors, Jews, and buccaneers, defy God and civilization, by keeping not the Sabbath day, nor wish for a day of rest, such as memory, youth and home, made hallowed.

V.

Thou shalt not think more of all thy gold, and how thou canst make it fastest, than how thou wilt enjoy it, after thou hast ridden, rough shod, over thy good old parent's precepts and examples, that thou mayest have nothing to reproach and sting thee, when thou art left ALONE in the land where thy father's blessing and thy mother's love hath rent thee.

VI.

Thou shalt not kill thy body by working in the rain, even though thou shalt make enough to buy physic and attendance with. Neither shalt thou kill thy neighbor's body in a duel; for, by "keeping cool," thou canst save his life and thy conscience. Neither shalt thou destroy thyself by getting "tight," nor "slewed," nor "high," nor "corned," nor "half-seas-over," nor "three sheets in the wind," by drinking smoothly down — "brandy-slings," "gin-cocktails," "whisky-punches," "rum-toddies," nor "egg-nogs." Neither shalt thou suck "mint-julips," nor "sherry-cobblers," through a straw, nor gurgle from a bottle the "raw material," nor "take it neat" from a decanter, for, while thou art swallowing down thy purse, and thy coat from off thy back, thou act burning the coat from off thy stomach; and. if thou couldst see the homes and lands, and gold dust, and home comforts already lying there—"a huge pile"—thou shouldst feel a choaking in thy throat; and when to that thou addest thy crooked walkings and hic-uping-talkings, of lodgings in the gutter, of broilings in the sun, of prospect holes half full of water, and of shafts and ditches, from which thou has emerged like a drowning rat, thou wilt feel disgusted with thyself, and inquire "Is thy servant a dog, that he doeth these things?" verily I will say, Farewell, old bottle, I will kiss thy gurgling lips no more. And thou, slings, cocktails, punches, smashes, cobblers, nogs, toddies, sangarees, and julips, forever farewell. Thy remembrance shames me, henceforth, I "cut thy acquaintance," and headaches, tremblings, heart burnings, blue-devils, and all the unholy catalogue of evils that follow in thy train. My wife's smiles and my children's merry-hearted laugh, shall charm and reward me for having the manly firmness and courage to say NO. I wish thee an eternal farewell.

VII.

Thou shall not grow discouraged, nor think of going home before thou hast made thy "pile," because thou hast not "struck a lead," nor found a "rich crevice," nor sunk a hole upon a "pocket," lest in going home thou shalt leave four dollars a day, and go to work, ashamed, at fifty cents, and serve thee right; for thou knowest by staying here, thou might'est strike a lead and fifty dollars a day, and keep thy manly self-respect, and then go home with enough to make thyself and others happy.

VIII.

Thou shalt not steal a pick, or a shovel, or a pan, from thy fellow miner; nor take away his tools without his leave; nor borrow those he cannot spare; nor return them broken, nor trouble him to fetch them back again; nor talk with him while his water rent is running on; nor remove his stake to enlarge thy claim, nor undermine his bank in following a lead, nor pan out gold from his "riffle-box," nor wash the "tailings" from his sluice's mouth. Neither shalt thou pick out specimens from the company's pan to put them in thy mouth, or in thy purse; nor cheat thy partner of his share; nor steal from thy cabin-mate his gold dust, to add to thine, for he will be sure to discover what thou hast done, and will straightway call his fellow miners together, and if the law hinder them not, they will hang thee, or give three fifty lashes, or shave thy head and brand thee, like a horse thief, with R upon thy cheek, to be known and read of all men, Californians in particular.

IX.

Thou shalt not tell any false tales about "good diggings in the mountains" to thy neighbor, that thou mayest benefit a friend who hath mules, and provisions, and tools, and blankets, he cannot sell — lest in deceiving thy neighbor, when he returneth through the snow, with naught save his rifle, he present thee with the contents thereof, and like a dog, thou shalt fall down and die.

X.

Thou shalt not commit unsuitable matrimony, nor covet "single blessedness"; nor forget absent maidens; nor neglect thy "first love"—but thou shalt consider how faithfully and patiently she awaiteth thy return; yea, and covereth each epistle that thou sendest with kisses of kindly welcome —until she hath thyself. Neither shalt thou covet thy neighbor's wife, nor trifle with the affections of his daughter; yet, if thy heart be free, and thou love and covet each other, thou shalt "pop the question" like a man, lest another more manly than thou art, should step in before thee, and thou love her in vain, and in the anguish of thy heart's disappointment, thou shalt quote the language of the great, and say, "sich is life"; and thy future lot be that of a poor, lonely, despised and comfortless bachelor.

A new Commandment give I unto thee — if thou hast a wife and little ones, that thou lovest dearer than thy life—that thou keep them continually before thee, to cheer and urge thee onward until thou canst say, "I have enough—God bless them—I will return." Then as thou journiest towards thy much loved home, with open arms shalt they come forth to welcome thee, and falling upon thy neck, weep tears of unuterable joy that thou art come; then in the fullness of thy heart's gratitude, thou shall kneel before thy Heavenly Father together, to thank Him for thy safe return. AMEN—So mote it be!

FORTY-NINE.

No. IV.

No. V.

SUN PRINT, SAN FRANCISCO

No. VI.

No. X.

Entered according to Act of Congress, in the year 1853, by JAMES M. HUTCHINGS, in the Clerk's Office of the U. S. District Court for the Northern District of California. Orders, pre paid, addressed "Box H, Placerville, El Dorado Co., Cal."

the as-yet-unnamed place that already was becoming more or less the official spot for visitors to gape at the Valley in astonishment, pronounce the view absolutely beyond description, and then set about trying to put it into words. "The fatigue of the journey had made us weary and a little peevish," Hutchings wrote, "but when our eyes looked upon the almost terrific grandeur of this scene, all, all was forgotten."

> We were almost speechless with wondering admiration, at its wild and sublime grandeur. "What!" exclaimed one at length, "have we come to the end of all things?"
> "Can this be the opening of the Seventh Seal?" cried another.

Above: Thomas A. Ayres's 1855 drawing, *General View of the Valley*

Opposite: Hutchings sold nearly one hundred thousand copies of "The Miner's Ten Commandments."

"This far, very far exceeds Niagara," says a third. . . . "I never expected to behold such a beautiful sight. This scene alone amply repays me for the travel."

During his exploration of the Valley, Hutchings busily took notes for a magazine he was planning to publish. The promised waterfall, Yosemite Falls, he noted, was not a thousand feet high; it was more than two thousand feet and "the highest in the world." (In actuality, it's 2,425 feet, highest on the continent and seventh in world ranking.) Eager to put his own stamp on things, Hutchings decided that the waterfall the Ahwahneechees called Po-ho'-no needed a more descriptive name. It looked, he thought, like a delicate veil waving from side to side in a breeze, so he dubbed it Bridalveil Fall.

While Hutchings recorded his descriptions in words, Thomas A. Ayres, an aspiring young artist Hutchings had hired to come along, tried to capture everything on his sketchpad. An astute promoter, Hutchings knew that Ayres's drawings, thirteen in all, could do more than his own verbosity in demonstrating Yosemite's unique beauty to the outside world. By the time they departed, Hutchings already had visions of Yosemite's future firmly in mind—and a determination that he would be part of it. On his way to San Francisco, he stopped in Mariposa and filed a report for the newly formed *Mariposa Gazette*, which he knew would be picked up by other newspapers across California and the larger nation:

> I have no doubt ere many years have elapsed, this wonderful valley will attract the lovers of the beautiful from all parts of the world; and be as famed as Niagara, for its wild sublimity, and magnificent scenery.
>
> We looked last upon it with regret that so fine a scene should be only the abode of wild animals and Indians, and that many months, perhaps years, would elapse before its silence would again be broken by the reverberating echoes of the rifle, or the musical notes of the white man's song.

Soon enough, Hutchings's *California Magazine* began circulating, with its lead article an effusive description of the Valley, backed by four lithographs made from Ayres's drawings. Ayres would make a return trip in 1856 to compile even more sketches and take them to New York City for a prominent exhibit that resulted in more orders for copies than he could possibly fill; he would die in a shipwreck in 1858.

Hutchings returned to the Valley in 1859, this time with Charles L. Weed, a practitioner of the young art of photography. Weed's photographs—twenty glass-plate negatives and forty stereographs, all the first taken of Yosemite Valley—were then copied as engravings to grace the front pages of *California Magazine*, which Hutchings boasted "will serve to immortalize the natural features of California, and draw from all parts of the world admiring tourists to visit them." Yosemite's secret was out.

◀◦▶

I went to the mountains to take my chances of dying or growing better, which I thought were about even.

—GALEN CLARK

AMONG THOSE WHO READ James Mason Hutchings's excited account of Yosemite in the *Mariposa Gazette* was a forty-one-year-old prospector from Dublin, New Hampshire, who seemed destined for a short life plagued by illness and chronic debt. By the time he was twenty-five, Galen Clark had already worked as a chair maker in New York, Boston, and Philadelphia; tried his hand at farming in Illinois and Iowa; and settled with his wife in northeastern Missouri, where drought and a leg injury made him unable to pay back a loan from his brother or the two hundred dollars in credit from his grocer to provide food for his growing family. He moved back to Philadelphia to paint houses, only to fall deeper in debt.

Opposite: Hutchings used his *California Magazine*, with engravings based on Charles L. Weed's photographs, to promote Yosemite's wonders.

HUTCHINGS'

CALIFORNIA MAGAZINE.

Vol. IV.   OCTOBER, 1859.   No. 4.

THE GREAT YO-SEMITE VALLEY.

CHAPTER I.

How it came to be Discovered.

"I see you stand like grayhounds in
  the slips,
Straining upon the start. The game 's
  a foot;
Follow your spirit; and, upon this
  charge,
Cry "—Ho! for the Yo-Semite!

THE early California resident will remember that during the spring and summer of 1850, much dissatisfaction existed among the white settlers and miners on the Merced, San Joaquin, Chowchilla, and Frezno rivers and their tributaries, on account of the frequent robberies committed upon them by the Chook-

THE YO-SEM-I-TE FALL.
[From a Photograph by C. L. Weed.]

Above: A tourist gazes down into the Valley from the Mariposa Trail, while Charles L. Weed, Yosemite's first photographer, takes his picture.

Opposite: Galen Clark, who came to Yosemite and the Mariposa Grove hoping to improve his failing health

When his wife died in 1848 giving birth to their fifth child, Clark placed the children in the care of his parents and headed for Texas, promising to send money for their upbringing. He failed again. The news of easy money in California's goldfields lured him from Texas to Mariposa County in 1853, but once more Clark barely scraped by, finally hiring himself out as a camp keeper for a mining company.

Within weeks of Hutchings's newspaper report, three different groups, totaling thirty-eight men, set out for Yosemite, the sickly and seemingly hapless Galen Clark among them. He was impressed by what he saw. At 8,836 feet, Half Dome was nearly three times the height of Mount Monadnock, the dominant feature of his boyhood home in New Hampshire. But he particularly liked some meadows along the South Fork of the Merced in a wooded, almost New England–like setting along the trail to the Valley, now called Wawona. In 1856 he filed an agricultural claim for 160 acres there.

At roughly the same time, Clark suffered what he called a "severe attack of hemorrhage of the lungs from which I was given up to die at any hour." It appeared that the troubles that had pursued him across the continent would overwhelm him once and for all. In his new surroundings, he decided to make the most of it. He went bareheaded and barefooted, on the theory that it would improve his circulation. He ate mostly deer liver, thinking that it might cure consumption. He was befriended by local Indians who often camped nearby, sharing their fish and their stories. And he rambled, loving "nothing in the world better than climbing to the top of a high ridge or mountain and looking off."

Galen Clark probably could have died a happy man at this point—still something of a sad sack, no doubt, given the string of misfortunes that had marked his existence; still a failure in the eyes of his family; yet happy at least to have found some final sanctuary from his sorrows. Somehow, Yosemite had restored him. The mountain air, he wrote, "exhilarates and thrills through every nervous fibre of the body, and makes the old feel young again. THE BRAIN BREATHES AS WELL AS THE LUNGS!" His health improved enough by 1857 that he built a log cabin, his carpentry skills coming in handy for

Halfway between the Mariposa Grove and Yosemite Valley, Clark's
Station became a popular stop for early tourists. The hospitable
Clark sits on the log at left.

making some simple furniture and a few bookshelves for his small but treasured library. He helped erect a bridge across the South Fork for the toll path that was now being opened to the Valley (two dollars for anyone on foot, one dollar for anyone on horseback—a seemingly inverted rate because the road builders, the Mann brothers, wanted people to rent horses from them), and he started taking in occasional travelers, who began calling his place Clark's Station.

Then, in the late spring of 1857, Clark got more than a health reprieve from Yosemite. He got a new purpose for his life. On a hunting trip with Milton Mann a few miles southeast of Clark's Station, he suddenly came across an extensive grove of giant sequoias—the world's largest trees, hundreds of them, towering mammoths, thousands of years old, their cinnamon-colored trunks lifting silently and massively above him.

At this point in history, the fate of such ancient wonders already seemed locked on a dismal trajectory. In 1852 Augustus T. Dowd had come across a similar sequoia grove while hunting a grizzly bear in Calaveras County, about a hundred miles northwest of Yosemite, in what is considered the *effective discovery* of giant sequoias. (Tough luck again for mountain man Joseph Walker's party, which had seen the Tuolumne and/or Merced groves in 1833, but got aced out due to the late and haphazard reporting of their adventures.) Dowd's news created a sensation in the mother-lode country, then in San Francisco, and then in Europe, once London newspapers caught wind of the story.

No one could believe trees so big, so tall, and so old existed. So of course the "Discovery Tree" was cut down: twenty-five men working ten days to fell the monster with a thundering crash that reportedly threw stones and dirt nearly a hundred feet in the air. They counted the tree rings and determined it had been nearly thirteen hundred years old. The remaining five-foot-tall stump was nearly ten yards in diameter. (In his travels to collect material for his magazine, James Mason Hutchings had attended a Fourth of July cotillion ball that used the stump as a dance floor, a drawing of which he happily included in his article, along with a lithograph of a bowling alley constructed on the trunk of a fallen big tree.)

The "Mother of the Forest" was next. Its thick bark was stripped from the living tree to a height of 120 feet and shipped to England, where it was reassembled into a tree (though hollow) for display at the Crystal Palace as dramatic proof that such giant trees did, in fact, exist. (Hutchings devoted an entire page of *California Magazine* to how the "Mother" looked with her bottom half stripped naked). Lumbermen followed quickly behind, dazzled by the prospects of how many houses could be made from a single sequoia twenty feet in diameter and nearly

No one could believe trees so big, so tall, and so old existed.

three hundred feet tall. They were disappointed that so many of the trees shattered when they hit the ground, wasting as much as 75 percent of the wood, and the remaining portion was ill-suited for construction because of its brittleness. But it could still be turned into fence posts, shingles, and even pencils—pencils from the mightiest trees on earth! By 1857 the logging of each new discovery of a sequoia grove was already picking up a momentum that would roll on through the rest of the century.

Milton Mann immediately saw the new grove he and Clark had stumbled upon for its monetary potential, too—as a tourist attraction to draw more business to his toll road—and he began extending a spur to accommodate the traffic. Clark, meanwhile,

Opposite: "The Mother of the Forest" in the Calaveras Grove had its bark stripped and shipped to England, where it was reassembled as a hollow tree to prove to disbelievers the size of California's giant sequoias.

Below: The Calaveras Grove's "Discovery Tree" was immediately cut down in 1852; they held cotillion balls on its stump.

LITH. OF NAGEL, FISHBOURNE & KUCHEL, 509 CLAY ST. COR. LEIDESDORFF ST. S.FRANCISCO.

THE STUMP AND TRUNK OF THE MAMMOTH TREE OF CALAVERAS.
Showing a Cotillion Party of Thirty-two Persons Dancing on the Stump at one time.
PUBLISHED BY J.M.HUTCHINGS, S.FRANCISCO.

A CORRECT VIEW OF THE MAMMOTH TREE GROVE,

By D. A. Plecker.

The engraving below represents correctly a Lithographic drawing of the "Mammoth Tree Grove," of Calaveras County, California, taken from a daguerreotype. If you have seen the trees which compose this beautiful Grove, you will remember with pleasure their sublimity and gigantic proportions. If you have not, you cannot fully conceive the beauty and grandeur of the scene, as the shadows of these forest giants fall upon the landscape. "They must be seen as they stand within their dark forest home, encircled by their smaller relatives, to be appreciated." These giants of the forest are situated fifteen miles from Murphy's Camp, on a ridge between the San Antonio branch of the Calaveras river, and the North Branch of the Stanislaus river, in latitude 38 deg. N. and longitude 120 deg. W. The altitude of the Grove is 4,550 feet above San Francisco, and 2,400 above Murphy's. Here, within an area of fifty acres, tower high above the surrounding forest eighty-five of these giant monsters of the vegetable kingdom.

As there are none like them known to man upon the face of the globe, naturalists have been at a loss to know what appellation to give them; and with what order to class them, their wood being of the nature of redwood or cedar, and their fruit is similar to that of the yellow pine.

The English naturalists have termed them 'Wellingtonia Gigantea;' the Yankees, not being willing at all to admit that name, have termed them "Washingtonia Gigantea," which appellation more properly belongs to them. There are 25 of these trees that will average over twenty feet in diameter at their base. The engraving represents the largest perfect standing tree, surrounded by a variety of other large trees of a different species. It is called the "mother of the forest," and has been deprived of its bark to the height of 116 feet, and at that height measures 39 feet 6 inches in circumference. It re-

sembles a mighty pyramid, whose base, including bark, measure 90 feet in circumference, and whose apex towers in the heavens to the distance of 310 feet. The average thickness of bark is one foot, and was sold to Mr. George Gale, who removed it, for the purpose of exhibition in the Atlantic States and Europe. This tree contains 500,000 feet of inch lumber.

The stump shown in the view, is the stump of the "Big Tree," which was cut down about two years ago. It is 8 feet high, and measures at that height 25 feet in diameter, without the bark. A saloon has been erected over this stump, the stump being its floor, on which large cotillion parties, and others who delight in such exercises, amuse themselves. It took five men twenty-five days to fell this tree, which they accomplished chiefly by boring.

There are other trees of the same species in this ever-green and ever-memorable forest, as large as the one shown in the engraving, but none so beautifully erect and symmetrical in every proportion.

There are various other trees in the forest which cannot here be described The father of the forest, which lies prostrate and buried one-third in the earth, measures at the base 110 feet in circumference. It is 200 feet to the first branch, the whole of which is hollow, and through which a person can walk erect, and in which is a never-failing spring of water, large enough to float a canoe. The estimated height is 400 feet. The "burnt tree" is also prostrate and hollow, through which a person can ride 60 feet on horseback. "As we gaze in admiring wonder upon these ancient *Californians*, that for 3000 years have withstood the storms, earthquakes, and volcanic eruptions of this mysterious land, we burn to be instructed in the fearful past, and anxiously inquire, 'who will tell to us its history?'"

Britton & Rey's Lith.

Ohio St. San Francisco

Entered according to Act of Congress in the year 1855, by D. A. PLECKER, in the Clerks Office of the U. S. District Court for the Northern District of California.

set about getting acquainted with the trees. First he made a painstaking count of every single mature sequoia. Not an estimate, a tree-by-tree count. There were 265 of them in the upper grove, and 241 of them in the lower. He measured their girth—forty-five feet in circumference for one of them—and marveled that they had all come from cones no bigger than a hen's egg. He learned from his Indian friends that they called the big trees *Wah-no-nah*, mimicking the sound of the owl they said was the forest's guardian spirit. They showed him another grove several more miles to the southeast, eventually called the Nelder Grove, which would soon be invaded by the lumbermen and stripped of many of its monarchs. Clark estimated five hundred mature sequoias in it when he named it the Fresno Grove; today only a hundred are left.

But the grove closest to his home also became closest to his heart, and Clark grew determined that this one, at least, would be spared from destruction. Some people suggested that it be named the Clark Grove, in honor of his "discovery." It's easy enough to imagine what Hutchings would have made of such an idea, but Clark, a modest man to his core, chose instead to call it the Mariposa Grove of Big Trees, after the county of its location. Friends thought he should at least have one sequoia bearing his name, and they put up a sign proclaiming it the Galen Clark Tree. He took the sign down.

Yosemite now had twin attractions—the Valley and the Mariposa Grove of Big Trees.

Those who knew him remarked on Clark's honesty and his gentle nature, on the straightforward gaze of his blue eyes, and on the way he tried to live by the teachings of the two books he had kept with him from the time his formal education ended a year after grammar school. He still consulted them regularly: a guide to manners and morals entitled *The American Chesterfield: Or the Way to Wealth, Honour, and Distinction* and the Bible. From the very beginning, it seems that his interest in the trees was not in self-aggrandizement, but something purer, something more appropriately proportional to the relationship between a mere man and a grove of gigantic trees that had been standing on that mountain slope, communing with one another, since before the New Testament in Clark's Bible had even been written. He would do what he could to see that those trees lived a little longer.

◄◦►

YOSEMITE NOW HAD TWIN ATTRACTIONS—the Valley, with its waterfalls and granite domes, and the Mariposa Grove of Big Trees. Clark's Station sat conveniently on the road to both, and with such a prime location an enterprising innkeeper might have made a pretty penny. Not Galen Clark. His health may have improved in Yosemite, but not his business acumen. When Yosemite's first photographer, Charles Weed, passed through, Clark apparently didn't even bother to charge him for room and board, and instead cheerfully guided him to his favorite spots in the sequoia grove. Visitors praised the food Clark prepared for them—speckled trout, poached eggs, rashers of bacon, homemade bread with wild-strawberry preserves—and many noted that he was an extremely knowledgeable host who "conversed well on any subject, and was at once philosopher, savant, chambermaid, cook, and landlord." But his prices, when he remembered to collect them, were so low that one tourist wrote: "I don't see how he lives." In truth, Clark was barely getting by. His erratic income was plowed back into supplies, into paying Indians to manage his crops and livestock, and into improving his buildings. But he was meeting interesting and influential people, exposing them to the Valley, mountains, and trees that had transformed his life.

By now, Hutchings's magazine and letter sheets, Ayres's drawings, Weeds's photographs, and the news of the Mariposa Grove had reached a larger audience, far beyond California, and more people had decided to see the wonders in person. It was hardly a flood of tourists—fewer than a hundred a season in the late 1850s and early 1860s—but they were noteworthy in that they, in turn, would make Yosemite even better known. Horace Greeley, the peripatetic editor of the *New-York Tribune* who famously advised the nation, "Go west, young man," arrived in 1859 on a highly publicized stagecoach tour of the West, in such a hurry that he endured a sunrise-to-midnight ride on "one of the hardest trotting mules in America" to see Yosemite Falls. It being August, the falls

were more trickle than torrent, a "humbug" in the eyes of Greeley, who departed quickly for the Mariposa Grove, which he deemed far more impressive: "the mammoths of the vegetable world" that were of "very substantial size when David danced before the ark." To Clark's delight, Greeley called for the trees' protection:

> If the village of Mariposa, the county, or the state of California does not immediately provide for the safety of these trees, I shall deplore [it]. . . .
>
> I am sure they will be more prized and treasured a thousand years hence than now, should they, by extreme care and caution, be preserved so long, and that thousands will then visit them, over smooth and spacious roads, for every one who now toils over the rugged bridle-path by which I have reached them.

In 1861 the photographer Carleton E. Watkins showed up at Clark's Station with a pack train of twelve mules, burdened with two thousand pounds of equipment: a bulky camera of Watkins's design with a wide-angle lens and capable of taking pictures up to eighteen inches by twenty-two inches; glass plates for his negatives weighing four pounds each; as well as tripods, chemicals, processing trays, and other cameras. Until recently, most of Watkins's business had been in baby portraits in San Francisco and large-format landscape photographs used to settle court cases in boundary disputes or as inducements to foreign investors for mining ventures. Presenting him with both artistic challenges and opportunities, Yosemite would turn Watkins into one of the West's most renowned photographic artists.

Above: In Carleton E. Watkins's photo of the entire Grizzly Giant, people standing at its base are barely visible.

Opposite: In this closer Watkins photo of the Grizzly Giant, Galen Clark seems embraced by the tree he loved.

He faced his first dilemma when Clark took him to the Mariposa Grove. How can a photograph even remotely suggest the astonishing size of a giant sequoia? Even if you're able to capture an image showing the tree from bottom to top—not an easy task in itself—the result is a photo depicting what appears to be a tree that is large but not particularly overwhelming. There's no recognizable sense of scale. Watkins solved the problem by having Clark stand at the base of the Grizzly Giant. The scale of a sequoia is immediately understood in all its stupefying hugeness with a human being placed next to it. In the closer photograph, showing perhaps the bottom twenty-five feet of the tree, Clark appears as if the massive swell of the trunk's butt might absorb him into just another gnarl on its bark. In the longer-distance shot that shows the entire tree (made possible only when Watkins

Above: Albert Bierstadt's *The Domes of the Yosemite*, 1867

Opposite: Bierstadt, center, paints in the midst of an Indian settlement in the Valley.

turned his camera ninety degrees to make it a vertical versus a horizontal image), Clark and a few companions are barely visible standing at the Grizzly Giant's base—Lilliputians to the tree's Gulliver.

Watkins moved on to the Valley, where he often photographed at dawn, when the wind and dust were less likely to interfere with the elaborate process of exposing a large wet-plate negative. Some of his exposures lasted up to an hour; a good day might include just four shots. In all, he produced thirty "mammoth" (large format) images and a hundred stereoscopic photos, some of which Josiah D. Whitney used to illustrate the California State Geological Survey's reports. Enhanced by repeated trips that produced thousands more photographs of the Valley and the big trees, Watkins's reputation soon

outstripped that of his predecessor, Charles Weed, as *the* photographer of Yosemite.

Copies of Watkins's 1861 photographs also found their way east to the personal collections of Oliver Wendell Holmes ("a perfection of art which compares with the finest European work"), and Ralph Waldo Emerson, and, more importantly, to a prominent exhibit in New York City. There, a young German-born, Massachusetts-raised landscape painter named Albert Bierstadt became enthralled by the images. He had recently made a name for himself with his dramatic paintings of the Rocky Mountains, but this—these waterfalls, these sheer cliffs, those trees—all but demanded that he come to Yosemite and the Sierra Nevada with his brushes. By 1863, Bierstadt had arrived at Clark's Station, then the Mariposa Grove, and then the Grizzly Giant, where Clark became the prop once again to graphically demonstrate the size of the trees he was now so closely identified with.

Bierstadt's artistry found freer expression in the Valley itself. He would produce at least fifteen oil paintings of it, including one, *The Domes of the Yosemite*, that was nine and a half feet by fifteen feet, and commanded a price of twenty-five thousand dollars, equal to the highest amount ever paid for an American work of art at the time. One eastern critic called it "the best landscape ever painted in the country." Bierstadt's success prompted scores of imitators, and on some summer afternoons in those early days, it's easy to imagine the soundscape of Yosemite being the light fluff of paintbrushes on canvas, the scratch of pencils on sketchpads, the click of camera shutters, and up in the sequoia grove a voice saying, "Galen, could you move a little to the left?"

The chain reaction that so often moves history was in full swing, the kind of sequence of people and events incrementally influencing each other that builds to a larger moment: the Mariposa Battalion, whose mission was to remove Indians from Yosemite Valley, inserts a statistic in a report that moves James Mason Hutchings to visit; Hutchings's first newspaper account activates Galen Clark, whose "discovery" of the Mariposa Grove (in conjunction

with Hutchings's relentless promotion of the Valley) attracts writers and photographers and artists, whose works reach larger and larger audiences. By 1864 a secluded recess in the Sierra Nevada that only a baker's dozen of years earlier had been unknown to anyone except the Ahwahneechees had become a topic of conversation in the newspapers and magazines of New York City and the subject of works of art displayed in salons across the ocean.

Still, not that many people had seen Yosemite in person. Would-be tourists needed to take an all-night boat ride from San Francisco to Stockton, followed by two dusty days by stage through the foothills to Coulterville, Big Oak Flat, or Mariposa, and then two or three more days of rough riding by

WATKINS' PACIFIC COAST.
26 Montgomery St., opposite Lick House entrance, San Francisco.

Galen's Hospice,

1168.

Mariposa Grove, Mariposa County, Cal.

Photographic Views of California, Oregon, and the Pacific Coast generally, embracing Yosemite Big Trees, Geysers, Mount Shasta, Mining City, etc., etc. Views made to order in any part of the State or Coast.

Carleton E. Watkins's stereograph of "Galen's Hospice" in the Mariposa Grove

horse or mule up and down steep mountainsides to the Valley's rim, and finally down what one traveler described as a "stairway . . . over loose boulders . . . where one false step would send horse and rider a mangled mass two thousand feet below." (The suffragist Elizabeth Cady Stanton refused to mount her mule for the treacherous descent, thinking it more prudent to walk, though it was the equivalent of twenty miles on level ground.)

Three toll roads (still more trail than road) had been blazed to the Valley—one from Coulterville and one from Big Oak Flat from the north, and the older route from Mariposa, which approached from the south and included the Mariposa Grove and Inspiration Point as extra attractions. Clark's Station sat astride the Mariposa trail, offering a night's

rest, good food, and a genial host who could be persuaded to pose for photographs and just might forget to submit a bill. To provide temporary (and free) shelter for the increasing number of visitors to his beloved trees, in May of 1864, Clark built a small cabin in the upper grove, which grateful tourists who rested there during a thunderstorm dubbed "Galen's Hospice."

Down in the Valley, two hotels had already been established: the Lower Hotel, below Sentinel Rock on the south side of the Merced River and opposite Yosemite Falls; and the Upper Hotel, about seven-tenths of a mile upstream. James Lamon, who had helped build the Upper Hotel, had filed a pre-emption claim on land farther up the Valley. He spent the winter of 1862–63 in a cabin there, proving for the first time that white people could live there year round. Here the chain reaction of history, as it sometimes does, makes a circle instead of a straight line. Hutchings had come to the same conclusion as Lamon. He had made a strenuous late-winter hike through deep drifts from Clark's Station to the Valley in March of 1862 ("A greater display of foolhardiness than were there displayed, never was exhibited in these mountains," the *Mariposa Gazette* opined) to discover the Valley floor relatively free of snow. Encouraged by that and by Lamon's experience, Hutchings now decided to make Yosemite Valley his home and business.

Having published his first book, *Scenes of Wonder and Curiosity in California,* Hutchings had sold *California Magazine,* invested and lost in a mining company in the Owens Valley, ridden a real-estate boom and bust south of San Mateo, and contemplated then rejected the notion of building a hotel near the Calaveras Big Trees he had so energetically propagandized. ("Such is change in California," he would have said.) And at age thirty-nine he had married the seventeen-year-old Elvira Sprout, who was now pregnant. Looking once again for a big chance, Hutchings turned once more to Yosemite, hoping to capitalize on all the publicity he had played a central role in initiating. He purchased the Upper Hotel—renaming it, of course, the Hutchings House—and moved in with his wife and mother-in-law.

Nine years earlier, Hutchings had predicted "this wonderful valley will attract the lovers of the beautiful from all parts of the world; and be as famed as Niagara." All that had come true. The open questions were whether Hutchings could now make a fortune from it—and whether Yosemite, still relatively pristine despite its fame, would suffer the same fate as Niagara. Those falls in New York State had once been pristine, too, and throughout the early 1800s had served as the new nation's premier symbol that the United States, though admittedly lacking in cultural attractions to match the cathedrals, museums, and ancient ruins of Europe, at least possessed natural wonders that equaled or even exceeded those of the Old World. But by 1864, Niagara Falls had long since become overdeveloped, crowded with curio shops and hucksters, its views marred by billboards and gaudy buildings. Now more carnival of commerce than cathedral of Nature, Niagara was smugly offered up by Europeans as Exhibit A of how Americans were still an uncouth and insatiably avaricious people capable of turning a national treasure into a national disgrace for the sake of a dollar. Would Yosemite be next?

3

THE DUTY
OF
GOVERNMENT

The enjoyment of scenery employs the mind without fatigue and yet enlivens it; and thus, through the influence of mind over body, gives the effect of refreshing rest and reinvigoration to the whole system.

—FREDERICK LAW OLMSTED

BY THE SUMMER OF 1864, the Civil War pitting the United States against the upstart Confederacy had entered its fourth blood-soaked year. Union forces under the command of Ulysses S. Grant were sustaining appalling casualties—18,400 in the Wilderness, 18,000 at Spotsylvania, 12,000 at Cold Harbor, 8,150 at Petersburg, all within the space of little more than a month—in Grant's grim determination to force the South to surrender at any cost. William Tecumseh Sherman and 100,000 troops were advancing on Atlanta, intent on defeating its 60,000 rebel defenders and laying waste to the city's industries and railroad facilities. A song written by Walter Kittredge of New Hampshire had become popular in both the North and the South, sorrowfully expressing the feelings of citizens on both sides of the conflict: "Many are the hearts that are weary tonight, wishing for the war to cease; many are the hearts looking for the right, to see the dawn of peace." Those weary hearts would have to wait yet another year for that dawn to break.

No place could have been geographically farther from the carnage than the quiet Yosemite Valley and the silent sequoias of the Mariposa Grove. But like everything else in America, they were connected to the conflict nonetheless—and never so much as that summer. Keeping California in the Union so its gold could help finance the war effort had been a priority for President Abraham Lincoln. Thomas Starr King, a prominent New England minister installed at San Francisco's First Unitarian Church and an avid promoter of Yosemite (he had written glowingly about the Valley in a series of eight articles for the *Boston Evening Transcript* and had sent Carleton Watkins's photos to Ralph Waldo Emerson and Oliver Wendell Holmes), tirelessly traveled the state. He used his patriotic fervor and oratorical skills to tamp down pro-Confederate sentiments that constantly sprang up among Californians whose roots were southern or whose aspirations foresaw a brighter future if the state became a republic of its own.

King's sudden death that spring saddened Galen Clark, who had hosted King in his home and shared his support for the Union. Remote as Clark's Station was, Clark followed the course of the conflict as closely as he could during sporadic visits to Mariposa for the mail. Two of his sons had enlisted in the army, and one had been killed in battle. In the album he kept in his cabin, mostly filled with pictures of the Valley and giant sequoias that grateful photographers had given him, Clark added portraits of President Lincoln and Union generals. But that summer of 1864, a camping party arrived at the South Fork of the Merced led by a man much more intimately connected to the president and the war's leaders.

Frederick Law Olmsted had directed the U.S. Sanitary Commission (the forerunner of the Red Cross) during the first years of the war, organizing a massive privately funded effort to improve the decrepit conditions in military camps and hospitals, where twice as many soldiers had been perishing from disease than from battle. It was a heroic undertaking and Olmsted had thrown himself into it, motivated by his intense opposition to slavery and his inability to serve active duty because a carriage accident in 1860 had shattered his left thigh bone, leaving him with one leg two inches shorter than the other. His work had brought him into direct contact with

Frederick Law Olmsted

Lincoln and his cabinet and generals, and he had earned their praise. Now Olmsted's administrative talents were directed at running the vast Mariposa Estate, a collection of mining operations employing thousands of people within its seventy-square-mile boundaries, encompassing a half dozen villages, including the county seat of Mariposa.

A wide chasm in social status separated the elite Olmsted from the humble proprietor of Clark's Station, but in addition to their fierce loyalty to the Union cause, Olmsted and Galen Clark had more in common than appearances suggested. Both men had led restless lives, switching from one occupation to another, managing to amass financial debts along the way. The scion of the founders of Hartford, Connecticut, and son of a wealthy merchant there, Olmsted had spent much of his life struggling to find a successful career, always ending up relying on his father's generosity when he started over on something else. He had given up on the dry-goods business, gone to China on a trading ship, completed a semester at Yale before dropping out, practiced "scientific" farming on Staten Island, taken a walking trip through England and Europe, tried his hand at journalism and publishing (which introduced him to Emerson, Henry Wadsworth Longfellow, Harriet Beecher Stowe, and other literary luminaries). But somehow Olmsted could never find something that might support him financially and gain him the kind of reputation his upbringing imposed on his ambitions.

Then, partly through his social connections (Washington Irving, William Cullen Bryant, Albert Bierstadt, and others petitioned on his behalf), in 1857 Olmsted was named superintendent of the effort to create New York City's Central Park, working with designer Calvert Vaux. In his new role, overseeing a work force that grew to twenty-five hundred men and more or less inventing the new profession of landscape architecture with Vaux, Olmsted discovered an innate knack for mastering complicated tasks

"You feel that they are distinguished strangers, [who] have come down to us from another world."

that demanded both farsighted planning and close, constant attention to detail. His genius at it took him from Central Park to the Sanitary Commission to the Mariposa Estate—just as his obstinacy in having things his own way ultimately contributed to him departing each job further in debt. (One friend, after praising Olmsted's "integrity and talent for organization," also noted "his impracticable temper, his irritable brain, his unappreciation of human nature.")

Olmsted and Clark shared something more: personal sorrow and chronic illness seemed to follow them both. Olmsted's younger brother—his closest friend and confidant—had died at age twenty-two after a long battle with tuberculosis. "Don't let Mary suffer while you are alive," were his last words, and Olmsted took it to heart by marrying his brother's widow and adopting their three children as his own. His and Mary's first child together died from cholera a week after the carriage accident that had crippled (and nearly killed) Olmsted. His health was never robust. A case of sumac poisoning in his youth weakened his eyes; jaundice, rheumatism, dyspepsia, and vertigo all made regular assaults over the years. But worst of all was his habit of working himself into a state of sleeplessness, worrying about all the details he wanted to keep in order, until he became physically and mentally exhausted. "He works like a dog all day and sits up nearly all night,"

Olmsted thought Yosemite Valley, captured here in a photograph by Eadweard Muybridge, was "sublimely beautiful."

one acquaintance observed, "doesn't go home to his family for five days together, works with steady, feverish intensity till four in the morning, sleeps on a sofa in his clothes, and breakfasts on strong coffee and pickles!!!"

"My brain and nerves tire so easily," Olmsted confessed to Mary. "I am incapable without excitement and excitement is so destructive to me." One cure he had discovered for his frayed nerves and insomnia was immersion in a beautiful natural landscape—from boyhood "tours in search of the picturesque" in northern New England to admiring the manicured public parks of Europe as a young man, to then finding tranquil respite from the frenetic bustle of New York City in the deceptively agrarian yet

man-made spaces he and Vaux were painstakingly designing in Central Park. Olmsted found solace again that summer of 1864, when he and his family and a group of friends encamped for three leisurely weeks among the pines and white azaleas on the South Fork of the Merced at Clark's Station. Besides the respite from work, there was the simple enjoyment of frolicking with his children in a mountain stream or gathering at night around a blazing campfire. Olmsted was further enchanted by the giant sequoias in the nearby Mariposa Grove:

> They don't strike you as monsters at all, but simply as the grandest tall trees you ever saw.
>
> You recognize them as soon as your eye falls on them far away, not merely from the unusual size of the trunk but its remarkable color, a cinnamon color, very elegant.
>
> You feel that they are distinguished strangers, [who] have come down to us from another world.

With Clark as his guide, Olmsted introduced himself to the "distinguished strangers," took measurements of their colossal trunks and miniature cones, and perhaps drew some peace and patience from the stoic presence of living things, like the Grizzly Giant, that over the course of centuries had weathered much fiercer tempests than he—and his nation—were experiencing.

The Olmsted party moved on to Yosemite Valley. From the overheated written accounts he had read of it, Olmsted expected to be knocked speechless by its vastness. Instead, he was charmed by its intimacy. Camped on the banks of the Merced, opposite

Yosemite Falls, with their tents precisely arranged so that their openings offered a vista of the lower fall, Olmsted wrote a letter to his father describing the river as "a stream meandering through a meadow, like . . . the Avon at Stratford—a trout stream with rushes and ferns, willows and poplars." What impressed him was not the individual superlatives of the size of the granite monoliths or the height of the waterfalls, and unlike Horace Greeley, he didn't grumble that the falls had little water in them. What struck Olmsted was the way *all* of the elements joined to create such an aesthetically pleasing whole. "Of course it is awfully grand," he assured his father, "but it is not frightful or fearful. It is sublimely beautiful, much more beautiful than I had supposed."

In Yosemite, he relaxed. He pondered the "quiet, pastoral groves, copses & swales of herbage" or the "soft tinted chalky quality of El Capitan." He watched thunderheads gather in the afternoon sky and then dissipate, enjoyed the play of soft colors in the Merced as it reflected Half Dome caught in the golden beam of sunset, noted a single shaft of moonlight piercing the Valley. "There are falls of water elsewhere finer, there are more stupendous cliffs, there are deeper and more awful chasms," he would later explain. "The union of deepest sublimity with the deepest beauty of nature, not in one feature or another, not in one part or one scene or another, not in any landscape that can be framed by itself, but all around and wherever the visitor goes, constitutes the Yosemite the greatest glory of nature." In other words, Nature had achieved in Yosemite what Olmsted and Vaux were hoping to approximate in Central Park: a landscape that was more than the sum of its parts, both exhilarating and soothing, a refuge for people like himself who needed to heal their tattered nerves or shake off whatever melancholy had overtaken them.

Olmsted topped off the trip by taking a guided journey with his twelve-year-old son John to the high country, where the nights were more bracing (the water in his canteen froze under his pillow) and the scenery, he thought, more beautiful than the Alps he had toured in Switzerland: "the grandest I ever saw." They ascended a 12,500-foot peak—Olmsted on his horse because of his bad leg, the others walking— and named it Mount Gibbs in honor of an old associate on the Sanitary Commission. From its pinnacle he could see the Mono desert to the east and glacial valleys in the Sierra peaks to the north and south, including, on Mount Lyell, "a snow bank six miles long in parts of which we could see the red snow described by Arctic travelers."

When Olmsted returned to work at the Mariposa Estate, where the mines were no longer showing a profit and the creditors were growing increasingly impatient, he was nevertheless revived. It was all thanks to Yosemite. And now came news from far away in Washington, D.C., that meant Yosemite would be an even greater part of his life, giving him the chance to repay the Valley for loaning him its rejuvenating energy and serenity.

ably years away, but "I think it important to obtain the proprietorship soon, to prevent occupation and especially to preserve the trees . . . from destruction." He suggested that Congress grant the Valley and the Mariposa Grove to the State of California "for public use, resort and recreation" and made "inalienable forever"—that is, reserved from private ownership for all time. Instead, the state would name a commission to "take control and begin to consider and lay out their plans for the gradual improvement of the properties."

What were Raymond's motives? We simply don't know. Perhaps he was moved by pure civic-mindedness, a desire to ensure that this special place not fall

EARLIER THAT YEAR, a letter had arrived at the United States Capitol for California's junior senator, John Conness. It was from Captain Israel Ward Raymond, the California representative of the Central American Steamship Transit Company in New York, one of the many outfits that made its money getting people to the El Dorado of the Pacific Coast. Included in the package was a set of Carleton Watkins's photographs of Yosemite.

In his brief letter, Raymond pointed out that a proper government survey of Yosemite was prob-

Above: Israel Ward Raymond
Right: Senator John Conness

prey to the haphazard ruination that had overtaken Niagara Falls. At the same time, Raymond could have been acting merely for the sake of his bottom line. Preservation of Yosemite's wonders would be good for his business: the more publicity the Valley and sequoia grove received as an unspoiled tourist attraction, the more customers the steamship line might book on their ships to California. (The Union Pacific, already in the midst of building a transcontinental railroad that would ultimately compete with Raymond's company, had underwritten Albert Bierstadt's travels to the West on the same grounds: the belief that his glorious paintings would increase traffic on their passenger trains.)

Equally unclear is whether the idea was Raymond's alone or whether his letter represented the thinking of a larger group. Senator Conness was certainly quick to act on the proposal and in later testimony asserted that "the application comes to us from various gentlemen in California, gentlemen of fortune, of taste, and of refinement." But Conness never named these men. An Irish immigrant and former piano maker from New York, Conness was a forty-niner who had prospected along the American River before entering California politics and only recently had taken office in the Senate. He was well connected with the state's elite, a diehard Unionist, and something of an idealist (his sympathies for Chinese immigration and their civil rights would

Never before had a nation set aside a large tract of natural scenery for the enjoyment of everyone and for all time.

run afoul of popular sentiments later in the 1860s and make him a one-termer). For all we know, Raymond's letter not only came as no surprise to Conness but merely crystallized a notion that the two of them and others had been discussing for some time.

Yet all that remains in the historical record is Raymond's letter, Conness's prompt filing of a bill in the Senate, and his allusion to "various gentlemen of California." But regardless of the motives behind it, and regardless of the number and names of its authors, what *is* certain is that this represented something unprecedented in human history. Never before had a nation set aside a large tract of natural scenery for the enjoyment of everyone and for all time.

Equally certain is this: the idea did not materialize out of the ether. It had its own seeds, which had been sown by others in the nation's collective past. That's the way history often works. Thomas Jefferson was neither acting alone nor uninfluenced by centuries of intellectual thought when he authored the Declaration of Independence, the radical document that created a new nation on the assertion that everyone possesses the inalienable rights of "life, liberty, and the pursuit of happiness." So, too, with the radical notion that some of a nation's most magnificent places should be preserved for all of its current and future citizens. In 1767, Jefferson himself had paid King George twenty shillings for Virginia's Natural

The gaudy tourist concessions intruding on the natural beauty of Niagara Falls had become something of a national embarrassment.

Bridge, a limestone arch 215 feet high spanning a gorge in a tributary of the James River. "I view it in some degree as a public trust," he wrote a friend, "and would on no consideration permit the bridge to be injured, defaced or masked from public view." But it was still private property.

In 1832 the artist George Catlin, traveling the Great Plains, was overcome by a vision that he would be among the last to see "the grace and beauty of Nature"; that pristine wildernesses were destined "to fall before the deadly axe and desolating hands of cultivating man." In a letter to a New York newspaper the next year, Catlin wrote: "What a splendid contemplation when one imagines them . . . by some great protecting policy of government, preserved . . . in a magnificent park. *A nation's Park*, containing man and beast, in all the wild and freshness of their nature's beauty."

Catlin's idea attracted little attention, but a few years later the New England Transcendentalists began espousing the notion that God could more easily be found in Nature than the works of man, and the natural world therefore deserved better treatment than their nation was exhibiting in its heedless rush to "conquer" the continent. "Here is sanctity which shames our religions, and reality which discredits our heroes," wrote Ralph Waldo Emerson in his essay *Nature*: "Here no history, or church, or state is interpolated on the divine sky and the immortal year."

Emerson's disciple, Henry David Thoreau, was more specific. "We need the tonic of wildness," he proclaimed. "In wildness is the preservation of the world." He called for "little oases of wildness in the desert of our civilization." The kings of England, he noted, had reserved forests to shelter their game for sport and food: "Why should not we, who renounced the king's authority, have our national preserves . . . not for idle sport or food, but for inspiration and our own true recreation? Or shall we, like villains, grub them all up, poaching on our own national domains?" Thoreau later wrote: "There is something in the mountain air that feeds the spirit and inspires. Will not man grow to greater perfection intellectually as well as physically under these influences? . . . Else, to what end does the world go on, and why was America discovered?"

Other voices would raise practical, versus spiritual, reasons to stop despoiling Nature's bounty. In 1864 a farmer and former diplomat named George Perkins Marsh, alarmed at how excessive logging had despoiled his native Vermont, leaving eroded lands and ruined rivers, published his seminal book, *Man and Nature*, now considered a landmark in America's conservation history. It warned that America was on the path of the Old World, where rampant deforestation had devastated the landscape and fertility of the Mediterranean, but it would be decades before his theories would take root.

Americans, de Tocqueville wrote, "will habitually prefer the useful to the beautiful, and they will require that the beautiful should be useful."

Whether or not Conness's Yosemite bill sprouted directly from any of these seeds, they had been spread across American soil for a number of years and were waiting for the right moment to germinate. At first blush, 1864 would hardly seem to be that moment. The fate of the nation itself, let alone its trees and wild places, was still at stake on battlefields littered with corpses. And no matter what Catlin and Emerson and Thoreau and Marsh may have been writing, the momentum of American history in the nineteenth century hardly tilted toward

conservation, a term that hadn't even been put into common use. Quite the contrary, the main business of Congress had been figuring out ways to dispose of public lands so they could be put to private use.

Jefferson had envisioned an orderly settlement of his "empire of liberty" stretching across the continent: the land surveyed into grids and parcels offered at auction by the General Land Office to yeoman farmers, with each new patent signed by the president himself. It hadn't worked out that way. "Orderly settlement" was not part of the American character. "Land hunger" and "land fever" were more apt descriptions. By 1832 the quickened pace of claims created a backlog of 10,500 patents awaiting President Andrew Jackson's signature to become legal; Congress passed a law authorizing a clerk to forge the signature so the disposal of the public domain would not slow down and the federal government, which relied on the sale of the public domain for revenue, could continue "doing a land office business." By 1841 so many settlers were pouring onto lands not yet surveyed that Congress passed the Preemption Act, which permitted squatters to purchase up to 160 acres of public land for as little as $1.25 per acre before it was offered at auction, if they could show a certain number of months of residence and a certain number of improvements to their claim.

The French journalist Alexis de Tocqueville best summarized the prevailing attitude of Americans toward their land. "In Europe," he wrote, "people talk a great deal about the wilds of America, but the Americans themselves never think about them."

They are insensible to the wonders of inanimate nature and they may be said not to perceive the mighty forests that surround them till they fall beneath the hatchet.

Their eyes are fixed upon another sight . . . the march across these wilds, draining swamps, turning the course of rivers, peopling solitudes, and subduing nature.

They will habitually prefer the useful to the beautiful, and they will require that the beautiful should be useful.

When the Civil War slowed the rate of expansion, Congress tried to stimulate it by upping the ante. The Pacific Railroad Act of 1862 promised vast tracts of the public domain to the companies building the first transcontinental railroad from Omaha to Sacramento. That same year the Homestead Act offered individuals their own 160 acres for free, if they improved the land and filed for their deed. Into this environment Senator John Conness planted his Yosemite bill, which proposed that Congress do the exact opposite of what it had been doing for all of its existence: save a piece of public land for the public instead of trying everything possible to sell it, or even give it away so it could become private property. So it could finally be made "useful." So it could be "redeemed from wilderness."

Conness obviously understood this when he introduced his bill on the Senate floor on May 17, 1864. "I will state to the Senate that this bill proposes to make a grant of certain premises located in the Sierra Nevada mountains, in the State of California, that are for all public purposes worthless, but which constitute, perhaps, some of the greatest wonders of the world." *For all public purposes worthless.* That was the first point he made, before tossing in a little nationalism that Yosemite and trees like the Grizzly Giant were also world-class wonders. Those sequoias, in fact, constituted a bigger selling point than the Valley in Conness's remarks. You've no doubt heard about them, he told his colleagues, recounting the story of the Calaveras Grove tree that was stripped and reassembled for disbelieving Europeans at the London World's Fair. The Mariposa Grove was even bigger, containing trees that "have no parallel, perhaps, in the world," he said, but "are subject now to damage and injury." His bill would assure their protection, "that they may be used and preserved for the benefit of mankind." Then, in case his fellow senators had forgotten his first point, he reiterated it: "It is a matter involving no appropriation whatever. The property is of no value to the Government."

In other words, it was something of a freebie. Congress wouldn't be spending any money and wouldn't be depriving its citizens of *valuable, useful* land (that is, good farm land, or merchantable timber, or precious minerals) by prohibiting private ownership. It helped, no doubt, that this was a place tucked into a remote recess of the Sierra Nevada. It

Carleton Watkins's photographs (above, from the area of Inspiration Point) were displayed in the Senate's Sergeant at Arms office to help persuade members that Yosemite Valley was a natural treasure worth protecting forever.

helped that Watkins's stunning photographs hung in the Sergeant at Arms office near the Senate chamber. It probably helped that at least one prominent business interest (and possibly more) wanted the bill to pass. And it helped that many of the senators knew that some of California's mammoth trees had been cut down, eliciting the scorn of those who already rubbed the degradation of Niagara in the nation's face; now at least one of the celebrated big tree groves would be preserved to show off to any disdainful Europeans who doubted America's superior natural wonders—or its capacity to properly care for them. It's impossible to look down your nose when your head is craned upward, looking toward the top of a living giant sequoia.

Virtually no real debate arose over the bill—a testament to Conness's political skills in framing the argument. One senator noted that the proposal was "a singular grant, unprecedented so far as my recollection goes," but he raised it as a question rather than an objection. "There is no parallel, and can be no parallel for this measure," Conness admitted, "for there is not, as I stated before, on earth such a condition of things. The Mariposa Big Tree Grove is really the wonder of the world." With that, the Senate passed the bill and moved on to other issues. A month later, the House did the same thing and sent the bill to the White House.

On June 30, 1864, President Abraham Lincoln had a lot on his mind. Confederate General Jubal Early had reached New Market, Virginia, readying his forces for a raid on Washington itself. Salmon Chase, the politically ambitious and perpetually petulant Secretary of the Treasury, had once more, as was his habit, written a threatening letter of resignation when he didn't get his way. This time, to Chase's surprise, Lincoln accepted it. The president had plenty of other business to take care of, besides finally ridding himself of an irritating cabinet secretary. He signed a bill increasing import duties and another broadening an income tax in order to continue the war for the Union's preservation. And on that day, whether he fully realized it or not, Abraham Lincoln took a historic step for a different kind of preservation. He signed a law to preserve *forever* a beautiful valley and a grove of trees that neither he nor the members of Congress had ever seen, thousands of miles away in California.

◄o►

AT THE MARIPOSA ESTATE, Frederick Law Olmsted had just returned from his family vacation when word reached him that the sequoias and scenery that had lifted his spirits were now entrusted to the State of California "upon the express conditions that the premises shall be held for public use [and] shall be inalienable for all time." He also learned that he had been appointed to lead the nine-member commission that would oversee the Yosemite Grant.

Overleaf: The act of Congress protecting Yosemite and the Mariposa Grove, unprecedented in human history, was signed by Speaker of the House Schuyler Colfax and President of the Senate, pro tempore, Daniel Clark; and became law with the signature of President Abraham Lincoln on June 30, 1864.

Thirty-eighth Congress of the United States of America;

At the first Session,

Begun and held at the City of Washington, on Monday, the seventh day of December, one thousand eight hundred and sixty-three

---

AN ACT

Authorizing a grant to the State of California of the "Yo-Semite Valley", and of the land embracing the "Mariposa Big Tree Grove."

Be it enacted by the Senate and House of Representatives of the United States of America in Congress assembled,

That there shall be, and is hereby, granted to the State of California, the "Cleft" or "Gorge", in the Granite Peak of the Sierra Nevada Mountains, situated in the county of Mariposa, in the State aforesaid, and the head-waters of the Merced River, and known as the Yo-Semite Valley, with its branches, or spurs, in estimated length fifteen miles, and in average width one mile back from the main edge of the precipice, on each side of the valley, with the stipulation nevertheless, that the said State shall accept this grant upon the express conditions, that the premises shall be held for public use, resort, and recreation; shall be inalienable for all time, but leases, not exceeding ten years may be granted for portions of said premises; all incomes derived from leases of privileges to be expended in the preservation and improvement of the property, or the roads leading thereto, the boundaries to be established at the cost of said State, by the United States Surveyor General of California, whose official plat, when affirmed by the Commissioner of the General Land Office, shall constitute the evidence of the locus, extent, and limits of the said Cleft or Gorge; the premises to be managed by the Governor of the State, with eight other Commissioners to be appointed by the Executive of California, and who shall receive no compensation for their services. Sec. 2. And be it further enacted, That there shall likewise be, and there is hereby granted to the said State of California the tracts embracing what is known as the "Mariposa Big Tree Grove", not to exceed the area of four sections and to be taken in legal subdivisions of one quarter section each, with the like stipulation as expressed in the first section of this act, as to the State's acceptance, with like conditions as in the first section of this act as to inalienability, yet with same lease privilege; the income to be expended in preservation, improvement, and protection of the property, the premises to be managed by Commissioners, as stipulated in the first section of this act, and to be taken in legal subdivisions as aforesaid; and the official plat of the United States Surveyor General, when affirmed by the Commissioner of the General Land Office, to be the Evidence of the locus of the said Mariposa Big Tree Grove.

Schuyler Colfax
Speaker of the House of Representatives.

Dan. Clark
President of the Senate, pro tempore.

Abraham Lincoln

Approved, June 30. 1864

I certify that this act did originate in the Senate.

J. W. Forney
Secretary.

Above: Olmsted advanced the money from his own pocket for the first survey and map of the new Yosemite Grant.

Over the past 150 years, speculation has abounded that Olmsted must have been involved in the effort to preserve Yosemite from the start. His name was among those Israel Ward Raymond had included as potential commissioners in the letter to Senator Conness that launched the legislative action. It would make all the sense in the world that Olmsted was one of the "various gentlemen of California" Conness alluded to on the Senate floor. Still, no documentary evidence exists suggesting that Olmsted had been aware of the proposed legislation, let alone participated in its development, or even that he had ever met Raymond. It makes equal sense that the representative of a steamship company, seeking to gain favorable action from Congress, would include on his list of recommended commissioners the name

of the former director of the U.S. Sanitary Commission and well-respected designer of New York City's famous Central Park, who at the moment just happened to be in California, in the foothills near Yosemite. It would be nice to know, one way or the other, but history leaves many questions unanswered.

Whatever the background, Olmsted acted quickly as chairman of the new commission. He sent geologist Clarence King to survey and map the Yosemite Grant (Congress had only approximated the boundaries: the Valley and its cliffs with a mile-wide border, and about twenty-five hundred acres for the Mariposa Grove). Because Congress had explicitly declined to spend any money on the Grant, and California had yet to appropriate any funds for it, Olmsted advanced five hundred dollars from his own pocket to get the survey under way. He wrote to Carleton Watkins and two California painters, soliciting their ideas, because, he said, as artists, "what affects natural scenery favorably or unfavorably to the enjoyment of mankind is the principle study of your lives." He began formulating his own ideas about how this experiment in protecting a wild public space should be managed—and why it needed to succeed.

Not that managing the Mariposa Estate wasn't consuming most of Olmsted's attention. Despite his best efforts, the estate was failing, the result of previous managers' derelictions and the unlucky geological fact that it lay a little south of the ore-rich hills that were steadily producing bullion and profits. A trial in New York exposed the fraud of the company officials who had misled investors and hired Olmsted with exaggerated promises of wealth. The bad publicity sent company stock into a tailspin, and with it much of Olmsted's pay. He was forced to arrange for creditors to take charge of the mines, and stepped down as manager.

In the spring of 1865, he began casting about for new work: maybe going back into journalism, or accepting an offer to run a drilling company in California's infant oil industry, or even joining Agoston Haraszthy, the "Father of California Viticulture," in trying to turn Sonoma into a wine-growing mecca. Directionless again, Olmsted became depressed,

overwhelmed by feelings of failure, consumed with regret for leaving his important post in the war effort for the chimera of California riches. "I can't turn my hand to anything," he wrote at the time, "and I've got no recognized trade—and I think that I am liable to break down entirely and suddenly." In San Francisco that April, when news reached the West Coast of President Lincoln's assassination less than a week after the war's end, Olmsted mourned with fifteen thousand others in a somber procession through the city streets. "I can't help feeling that the best part of me is pining here in a sort of solitary confinement," he confided to a friend, "and a man is never so lonely as in a crowd of strangers—even though a sympathetic crowd."

But there were flickers of hope. Olmsted supported his family with commissions generated by his reputation in landscape design: planning a two-hundred-acre cemetery in the hills above Oakland, submitting advice on the layout of the proposed College of California on the east side of the bay in what would become Berkeley, landscaping the gardens of two wealthy San Franciscans, and working with city leaders on preliminary plans for a large municipal park. Then came an invitation from Calvert Vaux, his old partner in New York, to return East and help design a new park for Brooklyn. Better than that, the overseers of Central Park in Manhattan wanted them both back to finish it. "I wish you could have seen your destiny in our art," Vaux pleaded. "God meant you should." Maybe Vaux was right. Maybe Olmsted did have a "recognized trade" after all, and it was landscape architecture. He agreed to take the two jobs with Vaux and made preparations for his family to leave California. But before he left, he had some thoughts on the future of Yosemite he wanted to share with his fellow commissioners.

Five of them gathered in Yosemite Valley on August 9, 1865: Olmsted; Alexander Deering, a Mariposa lawyer; George Coulter, founder of nearby Coulterville; William Ashburner, a mining engineer; and Galen Clark, who Olmsted considered "the doorkeeper of Yosemite." (The absent members were Governor Frederick Low, ex officio; Erastus Holden, a Stockton merchant; Josiah D. Whitney, the state geologist; and Israel Ward Raymond, whose letter had set things in motion.) Olmsted timed the meeting to coincide with a visit by a prestigious delegation from the East. Congressman Schuyler Colfax, the powerful Speaker of the House, led it.

Earlier that year, preparing for his well-publicized sojourn across the continent now that the Civil War had been won, Colfax had been among the last people to see President Lincoln alive, meeting with him in the White House on April 14 and getting a message to relay on Lincoln's behalf to the western miners who had played such a critical role in financing the Union effort. "Tell the miners for me that I shall promote their interests to the utmost of my ability, because their prosperity is the prosperity of the nation," Lincoln had said, adding that he would be urging soldiers now looking for employment to turn their eyes to the West. "How I would rejoice to make that trip" to California, the president

said, before asking Colfax to join him in going to Ford's Theatre that night. (Colfax had declined, but several days later served as one of the pallbearers at the murdered president's funeral, along with Senator Conness.)

Traveling with Colfax were a handful of influential reporters and some other important political figures. With the Olmsted family, they totaled nearly twenty people, the largest tourist group yet to enter Yosemite Valley. For a few days, they swam in the Merced, enjoyed the scenery, and sang Civil War songs around the evening campfire. Carleton Watkins showed up to take a photograph of them. On August 9, with the four other commissioners present, Olmsted read aloud the eight-thousand-word document he had been preparing, titled *Yosemite and the Mariposa Grove: A Preliminary Report*.

Like Senator Conness, Olmsted was acutely aware of Americans' predisposition to commerce, and, after describing Yosemite's natural beauty, he began his report by noting what he called the "obvious pecuniary advantage" of such scenery. Switzerland, he said, prospered economically from the thousands of tourists visiting the Alps. Their money supported inns and restaurants, provided farmers with "their best and almost only market" for surplus products, and fostered the development of railroads and carriage roads and steamboat lines and telegraphs that all contributed substantial revenue to the nation "without the exportation or abstraction from the country of anything of the slightest value to the people." So too, Olmsted predicted,

Frederick Law Olmsted (bottom row, second from left) and the
Colfax party of dignitaries who heard him read his prescient
report in Yosemite Valley on August 9, 1865

would the scenic attractions of Yosemite and the big trees become a financial boon to California and the United States. Scenery as magnificent as Yosemite's, carefully protected, would be good for business: the business of America.

But economics paled as a rationale for preserving Yosemite, Olmsted continued, compared to

The cover page of Olmsted's report on the future of the Yosemite Grant

something much more fundamental: the enduring promise of America and democracy. "It is a scientific fact," he asserted, "that the occasional contemplation of natural scenes of an impressive character . . . is favorable to the health and vigor of men and especially to the health and vigor of their intellect, [and] increases the subsequent capacity for happiness and the means of securing happiness." (Olmstead cited no scientific studies; he was more likely extrapolating from his own experience.) Knowing this "scientific fact," throughout history the world's aristocracies and richest families had set aside such places for their own exclusive benefit. "The enjoyment of the choicest natural scenes in the country and the means of recreation connected with them is thus a monopoly, in a very peculiar manner, of a very few, very rich people," he said. "The great mass of society, including those to whom it would be of the greatest benefit, is excluded from it." But the United States, Olmsted argued, was founded on a different notion than protecting the special privileges of birth or wealth:

> It is the main duty of government, if it is not the sole duty of government, to provide means of protection for all its citizens in the pursuit of happiness against the obstacles, otherwise insurmountable, which the selfishness of individuals or combinations of individuals is liable to interpose to that pursuit.
>
> . . . The establishment by government of great public grounds for the free enjoyment of the people under certain circumstances, is thus justified and enforced as a political duty.

A government of the people has the duty to protect its citizens' rights, including the *pursuit of happiness*, against the narrow and often powerful interests that would otherwise monopolize it for themselves. Like Lincoln in his Gettysburg Address, though not nearly as briefly or poetically, Olmsted had deliberately referred to the nation's most sacred document and then linked it to an idea that summoned its essence forward, expanding it in a way Jefferson himself would have understood and approved of. To reinforce his point, Olmsted began using the word "duty" as often as possible, over and over again, twice in some sentences, calling now on the patriotism and the deep belief in freedom and equality that had carried his countrymen through the horrific costs of the Civil War.

Next he got down to his specific plans for Yosemite. California needed to invest in better roads to the Valley and Mariposa Grove, cutting the time and expense of travel in half, so that the Yosemite Grant did not, by virtue of its inaccessibility, become a "rich man's park." Within the Valley itself, however, a more discreet road should be built, wide enough for just one carriage, making a one-way circuit up one side and down the other, keeping the meadows open for appropriate footpaths and a few bridges. All of this, he estimated, would cost roughly thirty thousand dollars. Another seven thousand would be devoted to completing the survey, advertising, paying

"This duty of preservation is the first. . . ."

a superintendent for two years, and constructing five strategically placed cabins (much like "Galen's Hospice" in the grove) as free resting places for visitors.

But none of this would be worthwhile without remembering another duty: to future generations and to the scenery itself. Regulations needed to be enacted and enforced, Olmsted said, to protect "the dignity of the scenery" against the demands of "the convenience, bad taste, playfulness, carelessness, or wanton destruction of present visitors." In a place as timeless as Yosemite, he declared, "the rights of posterity" outweighed the immediate desires of the present. Here, standing before what constituted a crowd in Yosemite Valley in 1865, when fewer than a hundred tourists normally visited each year, Olmsted cast his vision far over the horizon and invited his listeners to do the same:

Before many years, if proper facilities are offered, these hundreds will become thousands and in a century the whole number of visitors will be counted by millions. An injury to the scenery so slight that it may be unheeded by any visitor now, will be one multiplied by those millions. . . .

[T]herefore, laws to prevent an unjust use by individuals of that which is not individual but public property, must be made and rigidly enforced.

This duty of preservation is the first . . . because the millions who are hereafter to benefit . . . have the largest interest in it, and the largest interest should be first and most strenuously guarded.

A group of tourists posing with Yosemite Falls as a backdrop includes Yosemite commissioners Israel Ward Raymond (back row, third from left) and William Ashburner (back row, far left), who voted with Josiah Whitney to suppress Olmsted's report.

nation," an expression of "the will of the Nation as embodied in the act of Congress that this scenery shall never be private property, but that like certain defensive points upon our coast it shall be held solely for public purposes."

This is a startlingly prescient document, all the more remarkable because it was written so early in America's (and the world's) first venture into setting aside large tracts of public land, without any precedent for guidance. Here was Olmsted at his best. He had presented a closely reasoned yet farsighted argument about the future of Yosemite and all future parks, filled with democratic theory as well as practical recommendations, lofty ideals and the nuts and bolts of management—a manifesto combining the Declaration of Independence and the Constitution on behalf of public parks, binding them to the principles that had founded the nation now embarking on yet another experiment in democracy. Nothing like it had been written before. Nothing better has been written since.

Of the people gathered in a meadow near the Merced to hear Olmsted's report, a number were clearly impressed. Years later, in a letter to Olmsted, Galen Clark was still alluding to it and "the great object for which the valley was donated to the state." Albert D. Richardson of the *New-York Tribune*, part of Colfax's party, would write about the "wise legislation [that] secures to the proper national uses, incomparably the largest and grandest park, and the sublimest natural scenery in the whole world."

Since Yosemite should also be "considered as a field of study for science and art," he concluded, the makeup of the commission overseeing it should be changed, so that four members would be "students of Natural Science and Landscape Artists." Nor should the commissioners be solely residents of California. Yosemite, he proclaimed, was "a trust from the whole

Another member of the party, Samuel Bowles, publisher of *The Springfield Republican* in Massachusetts, was inspired enough by Olmsted's thoughts to propose more such parks. Yosemite, he wrote, "furnishes an admirable example for other objects of natural curiosity and popular interest all over the nation." New York, Bowles urged, should preserve Niagara Falls and a "generous section of her famous Adirondacks, and Maine one of her lakes and its surrounding woods."

Olmsted himself soon left California. For the rest of his life he would become involved in important works. He was commissioned to design seventeen major urban parks, the grounds of the United States Capitol, many campuses and private estates—even, appropriately, the effort to reclaim for the public and restore to its natural beauty the area around Niagara Falls, the place that had provided Congress with the starkest example of how commercial interests could ruin a landscape and embarrass a nation. Olmsted discovered that he not only had a "recognizable trade," he had come to define it. He was now known as the "father of landscape architecture." Yosemite had been crucial to that self-discovery. It would be natural, therefore, to think of Olmsted's report as the blueprint that guided the development of the new park and all the national parks that would follow. That would be natural and nice. But that would not be close to the historical truth.

No one at Olmsted's reading had disagreed with his proposal. Once he was safely out of California, however, three of the commissioners—Raymond, Ashburner, and Whitney—secretly convened and decided his recommendations were too expensive and too controversial to bring before the legislature. As head of the California Geological Survey, Whitney worried that the thirty-seven thousand dollars Olmsted proposed for the Yosemite Grant would cut into his own agency's chances for an appropriation. Such is politics; such is bureaucratic jockeying; such is history.

With the governor's concurrence, Olmsted's report itself was quietly shelved. Nearly a century would lapse before an Olmsted biographer, going through the papers of the Olmsted Brothers firm in Brookline, Massachusetts, in 1952, unearthed a copy of the report and published it. In the meantime, the history of Yosemite and the national park idea would need to proceed the way so much of American history has: not from a blueprint, however brilliantly devised, but by experimentation and improvisation, trial and error. Plenty of errors.

4

THE MORNING

OF

CREATION

Dear Sir,

Your report, which was at one time adopted at a meeting of the commissioners in the Valley, was suppressed by the combined action of some of the commissioners in San Francisco and the Governor, and never presented to the Legislature.

The State Geological Survey has worked for its own immediate interest in getting appropriations, and has worked against the interests of the Yosemite Valley. It would be better for the valley if these clashing interests could be entirely separated.

—GALEN CLARK TO FREDERICK LAW OLMSTED

WITH FREDERICK LAW OLMSTED back in New York City and his remarkably enlightened yet practical plan for the new Yosemite Grant thrown away or buried somewhere in a file cabinet in a state government office in California, the germinating seed of the national park idea had been deprived of the nurturing presence and wisdom of the nation's preeminent landscape designer.

Luckily, Yosemite still had Galen Clark. In the spring of 1866, the Grant's commissioners unanimously named him "Guardian of the Yosemite Valley and Big Tree Grove." He was handed an eight-page letter of instructions detailing his new duties: keep existing trails and bridges in good shape and build more; set up ten-year leases with the Valley residents and innkeepers who now found themselves occupying public land; prevent visitors from lighting careless campfires in the dry-grass meadows, Indians from breaking off oak limbs when harvesting acorns, and anyone from cutting down trees within the Grant's borders; plus innumerable other tasks involved in patrolling and protecting sixty square miles of rugged territory. For it all, Clark was offered five hundred dollars a year, which he could split with the single assistant he was permitted to hire.

Having just lost money investing in a petroleum company that went bankrupt, Clark probably appreciated the chance for a steady salary, but within two years the state legislature fell into the habit of not appropriating any funds for his pay or for the work that needed to be done. There was too much to do and not nearly enough money to get it done, aggravated by a cavalier, almost insulting attitude by lawmakers toward the livelihood of the employees entrusted with the job. Yosemite was already on its way to setting precedents that all future national park superintendents and protectors would face (and still do).

In his response, Clark would set a pattern for the future too. He carried on and did his best. He fulfilled his duty. He stopped local merchants from nailing advertising signs onto the trunks of his beloved sequoias. He caught two men who had cut down a huge pine near one of the hotels and dragged them to court in Mariposa, where they were fined twenty dollars each for the offense. Through his friendship with the Indians, who resented that the Valley had been taken from them without any recompensing

Galen Clark, Yosemite's first Guardian

payment, he persuaded them to resist breaking off branches of black oak trees. He built a bridge at the foot of Bridalveil Meadow and another above Vernal Fall. (The grateful commissioners steered some construction money to him from the hotel leases.)

After a series of heavy snows, high winds, and disastrous floods in early 1868, he embarked on snowshoes from Clark's Station (which had been crushed by an uprooted tree) on an arduous trek to inspect the damage to the Valley. There he must have felt like Job of the Old Testament when he surveyed what had happened to all the work he had done:

"All the bridges were carried away . . . the fences are mostly washed away . . . the ferry boat has gone altogether with the tree to which it was fastened. . . . Heavy drifts of timber and rocks have come over the falls; large trees broken, battered and shivered like pipe stems. . . . A large number of trees in different parts of the Valley are torn up by the roots . . . enough to make a million feet of timber."

But Clark's biggest vexation as Guardian came from the man whose writings had brought him to

Opposite: The sleeping rooms on the second floor of the Hutchings House were separated by cotton sheets at first, which complicated changing clothes by candlelight.

Below: One room was built around a big cedar tree, which became yet another Yosemite attraction.

Yosemite a decade earlier: James Mason Hutchings, the propagandist-turned-innkeeper who had taken over the old Upper Hotel a mere six weeks before the Valley had been declared "inalienable" forever. Hutchings's enchantment with Yosemite was indisputable, as was his central (if inadvertent) role in the chain of events that had led to it being preserved as a public trust. Equally indisputable was Hutchings's intention to turn Yosemite's wonders into a personal profit center. In this too, another national park precedent was being set. As historian Alfred Runte has said: "James Mason Hutchings loved Yosemite, no doubt about that. And every national park will have somebody who loves it deeply and then wants

to exploit the hell out of it. The thing about James Mason Hutchings is that once he gets control of Yosemite Valley, he does exactly what most concessioners do with a beautiful place like that. He begins to make it into another Niagara Falls. You have to pay him for the privilege of seeing Yosemite Valley."

Like everyone else with a building there, Hutchings was technically a squatter. The Valley had never been surveyed by the government and officially opened for settlement prior to the Yosemite Grant, and therefore Hutchings did not have legal title to the hotel and the land he claimed around it—a narrow strip that stretched from one side of the Valley to the other, like a private blockade. When Clark and the commissioners generously offered him a ten-year lease at one dollar a year, he disdainfully turned it down and convinced another early settler, John Lamon, to do the same thing. (Others in the Valley accepted the commission's offers.)

Hutchings had considerable political connections in Sacramento. Now he deployed them. In early 1868 the state legislature had passed a bill exempting him and Lamon from the law setting Yosemite aside. When the governor vetoed the bill, the legislature overrode it and asked Congress to ratify their action. In Washington, where Hutchings portrayed himself as a sturdy pioneer being unfairly treated, the House of Representatives happily went along with the exemption.

In desperation, Galen Clark reached out to Frederick Law Olmsted by letter:

Although the Legislature has done all in their power to throw away this munificent gift from Congress, yet we would appeal to Congress to not sanction their action in the matter, but to either compel the state to preserve it for the great purpose for which it was intended, or else as she has forfeited her right to it, to take it back and reserve it still as a National Park for public resort and recreation.

Will you not still so far take an interest in the matter as to use your great influence with the Congress, to have them protect this valley from the encroachments of private claims, that it may be forever kept free for the great public as a National Park.

It's worth digressing to note that Clark uses the phrase "national park" twice in his letter and suggests, as a last resort, that Congress take back the Grant and make Yosemite a federal, not a state, preserve. (It's also interesting that in closing his letter, besides sending his regards to Mrs. Olmsted, Clark offered: "If you need any seeds of trees growing near me please let me know and I will take pleasure in accommodating you." Imagine Olmsted planting a sequoia in Central Park.)

Clark's appeal prompted Olmsted to write an article for the *New-York Evening Post* and help circulate petitions to Congress opposing the House bill, which was effectively killed when the Senate Committee on Private Land Claims recommended indefinite postponement. To do otherwise, one senator said, "would be to give up the idea of the public enjoyment of the valley, and surrender it wholly to the purposes of private speculation."

The setback meant nothing to Hutchings. He simply ignored it, as well as the suit of ejectment Clark and the commissioners felt compelled to launch against him and Lamon in court. Instead, Hutchings began *expanding* his hotel, adding a workshop, another bedroom, and a combination kitchen and storeroom that became an attraction in itself, built around a stately cedar tree that dominated the interior space and seemed to emerge from the roof. Having learned from cold experience that his hotel received only two hours of sunlight in the winter because of the long shadow of the south cliffs, he also built a snug cabin for himself and his family closer to the Valley's north side.

He announced plans for more improvements. In the main hotel, where the sleeping rooms upstairs were separated only by cotton partitions, he wanted wooden walls, because guests complained that whenever they changed clothes by candlelight, their silhouettes were projected onto the cloth walls "hugely magnified, for the amusement of one's neighbors." He also began plans for two more "cottages"—one of stone, with two stories and ten bedrooms; the other of wood, with three stories and eighteen bedrooms—to accommodate more tourists.

With the state and federal governments at loggerheads over Hutchings's claims, and the lawsuit slowly working its way through the courts, Clark was powerless to do anything while Hutchings blithely thumbed his nose at the Guardian's attempts to assert public ownership of the Valley. Hutchings's only real impediment to his expansive plans, in fact, was the absence of a sawmill that could turn out the lumber he needed fast enough. In the fall of 1869, he bought machinery for one in San Francisco and had pack animals bring it to the Valley in parts, but no one knew how to assemble and run it.

At this particular moment, when Hutchings desperately needed a millwright, history took the kind of turn that sometimes seems more like the hand of Providence than the usual chain reaction of people and events. A young man showed up in the Valley looking for work. To Hutchings's great delight, he happened to be a mechanical genius with valuable experience running mills. To Yosemite's everlasting good fortune, the young man was really searching for a direction for his life, and his skills as a millwright would prove to be the least of his talents. His name was John Muir.

> The sea, the sky, the rivers have their ebbs and floods, and the earth itself throbs and pulses from calms to earthquakes. So also there are tides and floods in the affairs of men, which in some are slight and may be kept within bounds, but in others they overmaster everything.
>
> —John Muir

Muir was thirty-one when he took the job running Hutchings's sawmill. The long road that had led him to Yosemite Valley held clues to what he might eventually become, but it equally proved that Muir might just as easily have ended up somewhere else: if not a different person entirely, at least someone whose destiny would not have included saving Yosemite, invigorating the national park idea, and pointing America in a new direction.

He was born in a different country, in the bustling seaport of Dunbar, Scotland, the son of a downtown merchant whose extreme religious fervor and harsh views of both fatherhood and God meant that Muir, as the oldest boy in a family of eight children, suffered regular thrashings for any perceived lapses in obedience, including falling behind in his assignment to memorize verses of the Bible. The beatings, Muir remembered later, were "outrageously severe," and by the time he was eleven, he had "about three

John Muir in the early 1860s

fourths of the Old Testament and all of the New by heart and by sore flesh." The Muirs immigrated to the United States in 1849, settling on 160 acres of uncleared land not far from Portage, Wisconsin. There, Muir's father gradually became more interested in preaching his own stern gospel of damnation and brimstone than in farming, leaving the backbreaking fieldwork to his children.

As a teenager, Muir enjoyed rambling the countryside near the Fox River in his rare moments of spare time, but his greater passion was invention. He had a true gift for it. His first invention, as if a premonition for landing his job with Hutchings nearly two decades later, was a small-scale model of an automated sawmill, designed in the family basement with tools he had made from scratch. A wave of other inventions followed. He placed his bed on a fulcrum and attached it to a clock he had whittled from scrap wood; at the appointed time (one o'clock in the morning usually, so he could do his basement inventing before he began his farm chores), the bed turned upright and landed him on his feet to begin the day. He made water wheels, door locks, a homemade thermometer and barometer, and dozens of other ingenious devices—so many that at age twenty-two, following the advice of a neighbor, he left home without his father's blessing and entered some of these inventions in the state fair in Madison, where he won a special cash prize and a newspaper declared him a "genuine genius."

Encouraged by that success, and despite having suspended formal education when he moved to the

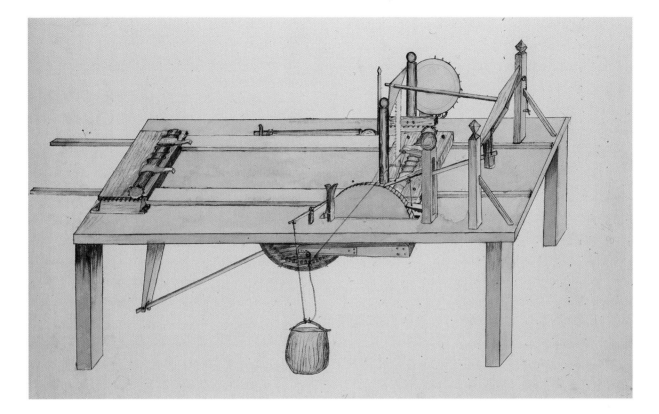

John Muir's diagram of one of his many inventions, an improved table saw

United States a decade earlier, Muir enrolled at the University of Wisconsin, which he attended off and on for six terms, focusing when he could on botany and geology. (Another invention helped in his studies: an elaborate mechanical "study desk" that automatically rotated the books he was reading at preset intervals.)

Muir's religious upbringing considered war morally abhorrent, and when President Lincoln instituted a draft in the Civil War (wealthy men could still buy their way out for three hundred dollars), Muir and a brother slipped across the border to Canada until the hostilities ended. In Ontario he designed a mill that could turn out rake handles and broom handles at a furious pace; back in the United States, in Indianapolis, Indiana, he joined a company making carriage wheels, where he impressed the owners with a time-and-motion study that increased the factory's efficiency and profits. He was still restless, filled with desires to explore the world or complete his studies of botany and geology, but in the midst of the nation's postwar industrial transformation, Muir was strategically poised to become one of its titans, not unlike Andrew Carnegie, a fellow Scotsman, only three years older, whose family had immigrated to America the same year as the Muirs. "Now that I am among machines I begin to *feel* that I have some talent that way," he wrote his sister in 1867, "and so I almost think, unless things change soon, I shall turn my whole mind into that channel."

A freak accident provided that change. Working on the belt of one of his machines, his hand slipped and the file he was holding pierced his right eye. He immediately lost sight in it; then his left eye went dark in sympathetic reaction. In his blindness, Muir felt suicidal "because I did not feel that I could have heart to look at any flower again." At best, he worried, he would live and die as an obscure statistic in the flow chart of some factory. Within a month his left eye was fine, and then his right eye slowly healed and regained its sight. His relieved bosses offered him a promotion, managing a new shop they were building. A partnership was dangled for the future. Muir could make more money for fewer hours of work, be back on track to make a name and fortune for himself. But during the month of darkness, a letter was read to him from his friend and mentor at the university in Madison, Jeanne Carr, an amateur botanist, sympathetic soul, and wife of one of his professors. It turned his mind in a new direction. "I have often in my heart wondered what God was training you for," she wrote.

Yosemite was nearly two hundred miles away. Muir decided to walk there.

He gave you the eye within the eye, to see in all natural objects the realized ideas of His mind. He gave you pure tastes, and the sturdy preference of whatsoever is most lovely and excellent.

He has made you a more individualized existence than is common. . . . He will surely place you where your work is.

Still unsure of his destiny, Muir decided that factories and efficiencies weren't it. An old dream returned. Maybe he would be an explorer, like one of his heroes, Alexander von Humboldt, and tour South America. To begin, he would walk from Indiana to Florida. "I wish I knew where I was going," he wrote Carr in September of 1867 after resigning his job: "Doomed to be 'carried of the spirit into the wilderness,' I suppose. I wish I could be more moderate in my desires, but I cannot, and so there is no rest."

With that Muir set off on foot toward the Gulf of Mexico, carrying three books (the poems of Robert Burns, Milton's *Paradise Lost*, and, of course, the New Testament) and a blank journal inscribed with his new address ("John Muir, Earth-planet, Universe"), ready to be filled with observations and sketches of the plants he encountered and collected. Two months and one thousand miles later, he arrived at the port village of Cedar Key, Florida, where the small harbor was empty of vessels that might take him to his real destination farther south. While he waited, a physical ailment intervened and once more redirected him. Malaria laid him low for three months. Then, during a stay in Cuba, he saw an advertisement for cheap fares to California, where a different climate might revitalize his weakened health. He already knew of a place called Yosemite— he had read a brochure about it in Indiana, and Carr had recommended it as a possible stop on his world-travel list. Muir decided to pay Yosemite a visit before finally settling on what to do next with his life.

Near the end of March 1868, he stepped off the steamer *Nebraska* onto the docks of San Francisco and, according to a story he loved to tell as an old man, immediately asked a carpenter on the street the quickest way out of town. "Where do you wish to go?" the man inquired. Muir answered: "Anywhere that's wild." The man directed him to the Oakland ferry. Yosemite was nearly two hundred miles away. Muir decided to walk there.

It took a month—a glorious month—crossing the Coastal Range at Pacheco Pass; wading through a sea of knee-deep flowers in the Central Valley (at one point he stopped to count the number of flowers within a square yard: 7,260 of them, representing sixteen species, not to mention thousands of grasses); climbing the foothills to Coulterville, then over a snow-covered trail to the famous Valley; and then over another snow-covered trail to the Grizzly Giant and big trees of the Mariposa Grove. At Clark's Station he met Galen Clark, who offered some bear meat to Muir and his traveling companion; his friend, by now rebelling against Muir's preferred traveling diet of tea and bread, devoured the meat, while Muir took only a small bite out of politeness to his host.

The Yosemite visit lasted only a little more than a week, and Muir wrote very little about it. He had marked his thirtieth birthday on the sojourn and was still planning the resumption of his grander exploration of South America, now that the mountain air had revived his health. But his immediate concern was providing for himself for the winter, and his brief introduction to Yosemite "only made me hungry for another far longer and farther reaching." He wanted to know the Sierra Nevada and its colossal trees a little better before setting out for the Andes. The only jobs to be found were where the Central Valley met the foothills. He harvested wheat, broke horses, operated a river ferry, sheared sheep, and then settled in for the dank winter in a "dismal little hut" near the town of Snelling, tending a herd of sheep for a dollar a day. At night he read Shakespeare, learned to bake sourdough bread, and made entries in his journal while contemplating his future. "What shall I do?" Muir asked himself. "Where shall I go?"

A practical answer came in the spring of 1869, when Pat Delaney, a local businessman, offered Muir a summer job helping herd 2,050 sheep up to the headwaters of the Merced and Tuolumne Rivers where they could fatten on the lush, alpine meadows. It would at least provide him with the closer view of the mountains, so he took the job. Trailing the swarm of ewes and lambs up the hillsides at a mile per hour, choking on the dust cloud they raised, and surrounded by an incessant "babel of baas,"

Muir became increasingly appalled at the damage the "hoofed locusts" did to the grasses and flowers in their path and increasingly disgusted at the rapacious economics of an industry predicated on the free destruction of the public domain.

Then, as they emerged into the high country, through an opening in the yellow pine forest he beheld the snowy peaks of the Sierra. "How near they seem," he wrote in his journal, "and how clear their outlines on the blue air, or rather *in* the blue air; for they seem saturated with it. How consuming strong the invitation they extend! Shall I be allowed to go into them? Night and day I'll pray that I may." It was June 6, 1869—the day John Muir felt Yosemite bend the trajectory of his life:

> We are now in the mountains and they are within us, kindling enthusiasm, making every nerve quiver, filling every pore and cell of us. Our flesh-and-bone tabernacle seems transparent as glass to the beauty about us, as if truly an inseparable part of it, thrilling with the air and trees, streams and rocks, in the waves of the sun—a part of all nature, neither old nor young, sick nor well, but immortal.

> I must drift about these love-monument mountains, glad to be a servant of servants in so holy a wilderness.

This was more than a restless young man finally deciding on a new direction. This was a profoundly religious experience, a moment of ecstasy and a revelation on the most fundamental level. Muir wasn't *choosing* a future to follow, that future was *calling* him to it. He understood it immediately in those terms. "How glorious a conversion," he recorded in his journal, "so complete and wholesome." He had witnessed the testimony of the rocks and would never be the same again. Muir referred to it as his "unconditional surrender to Nature."

In these mountains he called the "Range of Light," he wrote, "everything is perfectly clean and pure and full of divine lessons . . . until the hand of God becomes visible." That hand pointed in one direction: the realization that all of Creation is intertwined and on an equal standing; humankind is not *above* Nature but one part of a great, joyously interconnected web of being, where the rivers chant "an exulting chorus" and "the very stones seem talkative, sympathetic, brotherly." That realization—found during "the greatest of all the months of my life, the most truly, divinely free, boundless like eternity . . . one smooth, pure wild glow of Heaven's love, never to be blotted or blurred by anything past or present"—in turn pointed Muir to his destiny:

> I will follow my instincts, be myself for good or ill, and see what will be the upshot. As long as I live, I'll hear waterfalls and birds and winds sing. I'll interpret the rocks, learn the language of flood, storm, and the avalanche. I'll acquaint myself with the glaciers and wild gardens, and get as near the heart of the world as I can.

Opposite: Muir's sketch of Yosemite Valley from the top of North Dome, 1869

Below: Muir's drawing of his cabin shows how close he built it to Yosemite Falls.

When he came down from the mountains at the end of the summer, instead of heading for San Francisco and a ship to take him to South America, Muir went to the Yosemite Valley, looking for a way to support himself for the winter in "the grandest of all the special temples of Nature I was ever permitted to enter . . . the sanctum sanctorum of the Sierra." There, James Mason Hutchings just happened to be looking for someone with a little sawmill experience.

◄◦►

HISTORY ABOUNDS with coincidences and ironies, but not many of them top the two associated with John Muir's first connections to Yosemite—that therefore made possible the passionate voice that would ultimately save Yosemite and inspire millions of Americans to preserve rather than exploit Nature's sacred bounties. What brought him to the "Range of

Cabin in Yo. Val. 1869

Light" was a herd of voracious sheep, which he tended as it despoiled Tuolumne Meadows. And what first kept him in the "sanctum sanctorum of the Sierra" was a water-powered sawmill, which he built and ran, whose steady whine echoed off the walls of Yosemite Valley for two years as it turned pine trees into two-by-fours and sawdust.

In building the sawmill and putting its machinery to work for the many projects Hutchings wanted, Muir was careful, at least, to use only the trees that had already been toppled by the disastrous storms of the winter of 1867–68, although he dammed Yosemite Creek near the base of the falls and dug a millrace to power the waterwheel. Soon enough, Hutchings's hotel had proper wooden partitions instead of sheets to separate its rooms, the "cabins" were completed for extra tourists, and the Big Tree Room was improved. For himself and a coworker, Muir also built a one-room cabin near the base of Yosemite Falls. Its one window framed a view of the falls, its floor had spaces to permit ferns to grow, and another small ditch he dug diverted some of the stream through one corner of the hut so that at night, while he slept in a hammock suspended from the rafters, Muir could hear the water "sing and warble in low, sweet tones." He bragged that the cabin cost him a total of three or four dollars (a tiny fraction of the twenty-eight dollars Henry David Thoreau had expended on his cabin at Walden Pond) and was "the handsomest building in the Valley."

But Muir was not there to make a living. His work for Hutchings was a means to an end, and the end was exploring everything Yosemite had to offer. Nothing escaped his observation and his contemplation, from a tiny drop of dew on an alder bush he scrutinized with his pocket lens to the way sugar pines "toss out their immense arms in what might seem extravagant gestures . . . the priests of pines [that] seem ever to be addressing the surrounding forest"; from the lines and scratches on the granite domes ("glacial hieroglyphics whose interpretation is the reward of all who devoutly study them") to the sound (the "spontaneous, irrepressible gladness") of his favorite bird, the tiny water ouzel, "who could no more help giving out sweet song than a rose sweet fragrance." Like Muir himself, "he must sing, though the heavens fall."

He became fascinated with sequoias, the "noblest of God's trees," and spent days examining their thick bark, small cones, and minuscule seeds; measuring their massive trunks and smallest branches; estimating their ages by counting the rings on fallen monarchs; noting a 380-year-old silver fir growing in a straight ditch created by one of the giants when it fell more than a thousand years earlier; realizing, by careful inspection of a freshly scorched plot of ground and the many sequoia saplings on it, that fire was somehow an integral part of the species' renewal; and finding meaning from the "curious fact that all the very old sequoias had lost their heads by lightning stroke." He saw both scientific and metaphorical significance in that fact. "Most of the Sierra trees die of disease, insects, fungi, etc.," he observed, "but nothing hurts the big tree. . . . Barring

Muir's sketch of his precarious perch on the lip of Upper Yosemite Fall

accidents, it seems to be immortal. . . . Of all living things, sequoia is perhaps the only one able to wait long enough to make sure of being struck by lightning." Muir's immersion was so complete he sometimes used the sequoia's purple sap as ink for writing letters. He even soaked sequoia cones in water and drank the liquid "to improve my color," he said, "and render myself more tree-wise and sequoical."

Caught in his combination of scientific curiosity, boyish enthusiasm, and religious rapture, Muir took insane risks and survived freak accidents. He edged out along the lip of Upper Yosemite Fall, within a few feet of the foaming water, where it plunges more than a thousand vertical feet, simply to hear "the death song of Yosemite Creek." He tied himself to the tip of a hundred-foot Douglas fir to ride out a raging storm, "free to take the wind into my pulses" and listening to "the Aeolian music of its topmost needles" as it swayed in the gale. One night, he wedged himself into a small declivity in the granite at the base of Yosemite Falls to observe a full moon through the thundering cascade; one particularly cold winter, he attempted to climb the four-hundred-foot ice cone that formed at the falls' base, barely escaping death when a mass of falling ice just missed him. He could have perished again when an avalanche swept him down a side canyon (he had wallowed up it in waist-deep snow the entire day, hoping to reach the summit so he could enjoy the sunset); miraculously unscathed, he called it "the most spiritual and exhilarating of all the modes of motion I have ever experienced."

At two-thirty early one March morning, a great earthquake shook Yosemite Valley, a series of jolts and shocks so violent, Muir wrote, that when he ran out from his cabin (shouting "noble earthquake!") the ground was so unstable "that I had to balance myself carefully in walking, as if on the deck of a ship among waves." Half a mile away, massive Eagle Rock gave way from the south wall with a tremendous roar, and he saw it tumble in thousands of huge boulders. While the few other winter residents were trembling in panic, his reaction was pure John Muir:

> Eager to examine the new-born talus I ran up the Valley in the moonlight and climbed upon it before the huge blocks, after their fiery flight, had come to complete rest. They were slowly settling into their places, chafing, grating against one another, groaning, and whispering. . . .
>
> A cloud of dust particles, lighted by the moon, floated across the whole breadth of the Valley . . . and the air was filled with the odor of crushed Douglas

spruces from a grove that had been mowed down and mashed like weeds.

Understandably, many people began viewing Muir as something of an eccentric. When he met a total stranger deep in a Sierra forest and said he was there to commune with the trees, the stranger looked at the gaunt man with the blazing blues eyes and long beard and replied: "Oh, then, you must be John Muir." But he was more than a tree-hugger. He was a scientist, as capable of filling his notebooks with pages of precise descriptions of plants (using their Latin binomials) as he was with rapturous prose. His interest in geology, especially the young science of glaciology, became as consuming as his seeming pantheism.

As his work in Hutchings's sawmill wound down, he had more time for longer excursions into the Sierra, which he came to know more intimately than anyone. He traveled light—just some bread, tea, and sugar for provisions—and slept on a bed of pine boughs, thinking nothing of covering fifty miles in two days. He bought an ice axe and hobnailed boots and attempted more difficult ascents of the highest peaks in the region, including the first known summiting of 13,156-foot Mount Ritter.

Everywhere Muir looked, he saw evidence that the landscape had been shaped by glaciers—high up in the mountain recesses he even discovered a glacier still at work—and in contemplating their handiwork, he found not a contradiction to his deeply held religious beliefs, but their confirmation. "One learns," he concluded, "that the world, though made, is yet being made. That this is still the morning of

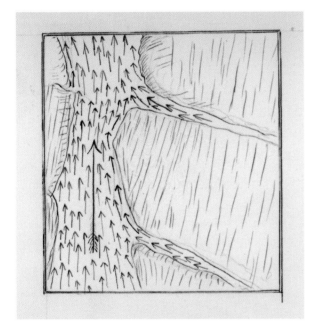

Muir drew arrows to show the direction of the glacier flow he
believed shaped Half Dome.

creation." God was everywhere, working through the natural world, and everything was connected, even across eons of time:

> If among the agents that Nature has employed in making these mountains there be one that above all others deserves the name of Destroyer, it is the glacier. But we quickly learn that destruction is creation. . . .
>
> Nature is ever at work building and pulling down, creating and destroying, keeping everything whirling and flowing, allowing no rest but in rhythmical motion, chasing everything in endless song out of one beautiful form into another.

Even Yosemite Valley itself, Muir said, had been carved and polished by glaciers—an assertion that brought him into direct conflict with Josiah D. Whitney, California's state geologist, who insisted on a theory that it was obviously the result of a cataclysmic collapse of the Valley's floor. Whitney huffily dismissed Muir's notions as the nonsense of a "mere sheepherder" and "ignoramus," and by virtue of his reputation kept most other professional geologists in his camp. Muir stuck to his guns, however, and would go on to catalog sixty-five glaciers in the Sierra. Not until the early twentieth century, as the science of geology advanced, did the verdict finally come down: there had been at least three glacial periods (not one, as Muir had believed), and the Valley had been started by river action before the glaciers arrived to finish the job. But the cataclysmic collapse was pure fantasy, and Muir "was more nearly right . . . than any professional geologist of his time."

Geologist Josiah D. Whitney

(Whitney becomes easy to dislike in the story of Yosemite's early days: with bureaucratic elbow-throwing, he participated in suppressing Frederick Law Olmsted's brilliant report, and out of haughty arrogance he denigrated John Muir while being absolutely wrong about the first question anyone asks when they encounter Yosemite: "How did this incredible Valley come into being?" But in fairness, Whitney did an admirable job as head of the state's geological survey, assembling an impressive team of scientists to conduct it and fighting off political forces that viewed the work as principally a scouting mission to locate precious metals on behalf of well-connected insiders. He was also among the first to refer to "the Yosemite National Park" in a book he published in 1868. Not for nothing was the highest peak in the Lower 48 named for him.)

Muir's relationship with his employer, James Mason Hutchings, became equally contentious. Hutchings resented the affection his wife and three children had for the friendly Scotsman who loved regaling any audience with stories. More than that, as the self-designated "expert" on Yosemite, Hutchings grew jealous of Muir's rising popularity with the tourists. A steamy novel, *Zanita: A Tale of the Yo-sem-ite*, written by an Irish countess who spent a summer at the Hutchings House, included a character named Kenmuir, an intense man of the mountains ("His open blue eyes of honest questioning, and glorious auburn hair might have stood as a portrait of the angel Raphael") who had become, in effect, one of the attractions of area. The book only enhanced Muir's cachet. More and more people started asking for him to be their Yosemite guide instead of the man who considered it his private domain.

Among them was none other than Muir's Transcendentalist hero, Ralph Waldo Emerson, who showed up in 1871 with a dozen traveling companions, most of them much younger than the sixty-eight-year-old Sage of Concord. As he and his entourage rode horseback to many of the sights, the acolytes seemed to vie with one another for the great man's approval: one of them quoted "The Wreck of the Hesperus" at Vernal Fall; Dante, Michelangelo, and Machiavelli were the topics at Nevada

Fall; Mirror Lake prompted someone to recite maxims from Goethe; the evening discussion centered on Boccaccio's *Decameron*. Then a letter from "a young man, living in the valley, and tending the sawmill" was delivered, inviting Emerson to pay a visit. Intrigued, he accepted and the next day came for a tour of the tiny loft in the sawmill Muir now called home (a peeved Hutchings had given the cabin to someone else while Muir was on a mountain trip). Here was a man living out what Emerson had been

Ralph Waldo Emerson

After Emerson gave the Samoset Tree its name, Muir sketched it in his journal. "You are yourself a sequoia," he told the old philosopher.

preaching—not merely an intellectual contemplation of Divinity found through Nature but something much more organic and visceral; here was someone who had plugged himself directly into the currents of the cosmos, firmly believing that "every one of its living creatures . . . and every crystal of its rocks . . . is throbbing and pulsing with the heartbeats of God." Emerson himself could not have said it better.

Over the next few days the old Transcendentalist returned for more visits, and the two men formed something of a bond, more bemused father and eager son than a friendship between equals, but when Emerson's group set off for the sequoias, Muir rode next to him by invitation. For a while they talked "on literary points," one of the young companions sniffed, adding, "M. was not strong here." Then Muir provided a traveling seminar on trees, "and we grew learned and were able to tell a sugar pine from a yellow pine, and to name a silver fir."

Galen Clark was honored to accompany such an eminent fellow New Englander to the Mariposa Grove and asked Emerson to give one of the sequoias a name; Emerson chose Samoset, in honor of the Indian who had greeted the Pilgrims at Plymouth Rock. They lined up thirteen horses around the base of the Grizzly Giant and estimated it would take six more to close the circle. "The greatest wonder," Emerson said, "is that we can see these trees and not wonder more."

Muir beseeched the old man to spend the night with him among the sequoias, promising to build "a glorious campfire" so that "the great trees would stand about us transfigured in the purple light." But the group, Muir wrote, "was full of indoor philosophy" and vetoed the plan. "You are yourself a sequoia," Muir begged Emerson directly. "Stop and get acquainted with your big brethren." Again, the answer was no. (Thirty years later, Muir was still complaining about the missed opportunity, laying the blame on Emerson's "affectionate but sadly civilized friends, who seemed as full of old-fashioned conformity as of bold intellectual independence.") As the group rode off toward civilization, Emerson lagged behind and waved a last goodbye with his hat before disappearing over a ridge. Muir, downhearted, returned to the sanctuary of the grove, built himself a bed of "sequoia plumes and ferns," made a big fire, and "though lonesome for the first time in these forests, I quickly took heart again—the trees had not gone to Boston, nor the birds."

◄◦►

GALEN CLARK ALSO HAD NOT gone to Boston. He was, Muir wrote, "the best mountaineer I ever met"—high praise from a man who seemed half-goat himself. Their friendship, begun three years earlier during Muir's brief first trip to the region, and their mutual love of Yosemite and the Sierra were deepened on three extended excursions they took together: one to explore the Big Tuolumne Canyon up from Hetch Hetchy Valley; another to help Muir establish a line of wooden stakes on McClure Glacier to measure its movement (during which they

also climbed Mount Lyell); and another to check out the mountains south of Yosemite near the headwaters of the Kings River.

Taller, thinner, and more than twenty years younger, Muir could scramble along riverbeds and up talus slopes faster than Clark, while the Guardian was better at bulling through thick brush. "His pot was always the first to boil" when preparing tea or porridge, Muir wrote admiringly, but he was "utterly careless about his beds," willing to lie down on bare rocks for the night, "saying that his own bones were as hard as any stones and could do him no harm." Hard bones, perhaps, but not a hard heart. Clark was, Muir thought, "one of the kindest and most amiable of all my mountain friends." Unlike the outgoing Muir, who relished merriment and mirth around the campfire, Clark "never indulged in boisterous laughter," his friend wrote, "however deep and fun-provoking a story might be." But "I never heard him utter a hasty, angry, fault-finding word" and "from his hospitable well-supplied cabin no weary wanderer ever went away hungry or unrested."

If he envied Muir's growing celebrity, Clark characteristically kept it to himself. He had a job to do and the job came first. "I do not tell stories, but will answer questions," Clark once told a guest. "I am not a spurting, gushing geyser of information. I am not an artesian well, but I can be pumped." Geyser or not, he remained, in Muir's view, "one of the most sincere tree-lovers I ever knew."

And now Clark, too, would be left alone with the trees, just as Muir had been when Emerson

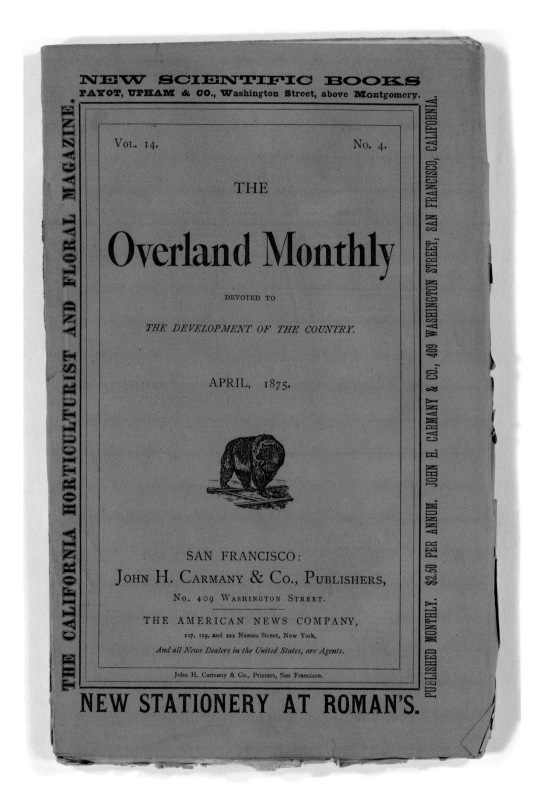

Vol. 14.   No. 4.

THE

Overland Monthly

DEVOTED TO

THE DEVELOPMENT OF THE COUNTRY.

APRIL, 1875.

SAN FRANCISCO:

JOHN H. CARMANY & CO., PUBLISHERS,

No. 409 WASHINGTON STREET.

THE AMERICAN NEWS COMPANY,

117, 119, and 121 Nassau Street, New York,

And all News Dealers in the United States, are Agents.

John H. Carmany & Co., Printers, San Francisco.

departed. In late 1873, Muir moved to Oakland. In addition to his talents as an inventor, as a scientist, and as an exquisite tuning fork to the music of Nature, he was also an eloquent writer, filled as he was with the majestic cadences of the King James Bible he had been forced to memorize. He had recently demonstrated his skill in some articles about Yosemite's glaciers for Horace Greeley's *New-York Daily Tribune*. Some geologist acquaintances were urging him to turn his glacial studies into a formal book. Emerson sent a letter saying that Muir now needed to leave his "mountain tabernacle" and come east to write and teach. Muir's mentor, Jeanne Carr, believed he needed a larger forum than the groups of tourists who encountered him in the Valley. Muir was coming to the same conclusion:

How little note is taken of the deeds of Nature! What paper publishes her reports? . . . Who publishes the sheet-music of the winds, or the written music of water written in river-lines? Who reports the works and ways of the clouds, those wondrous creations coming into being every day like freshly upheaved mountains?

To best preserve for others what he had discovered for himself in Yosemite, Muir would need to "preach Nature like an apostle." And to reach the largest congregation, he would need to spend more time behind a writing desk, crafting his sermons. The trade-off would mean less time in the mountains and forests, communing directly with the sacredness he had found there. Muir was flattered by the scientists' call for an academic work on glaciers and by Emerson's invitation to join "*the better men* of New England," but he had no intention of taking that advice. In Oakland he began work on a series of articles for *The Overland Monthly*, hoping to reach a broad audience and still permit himself opportunities from time to time to return to the Valley, the big trees, and the Range of Light. Yosemite would never again be his permanent home. Yet he would never really leave it.

Opposite: Muir's article "Wild Wool" appeared in the April 1875 edition of *The Overland Monthly*.

5

PERVERSION
OF THE
TRUST

Like anything else worth while, from the very beginning,
however well guarded, [parks] have always been subject to attack
by despoiling gain-seekers and mischief-makers of every degree
from Satan to Senators, eagerly trying to make everything
immediately and selfishly commercial.

—JOHN MUIR

THE YOSEMITE GRANT was nearing its tenth anniversary when John Muir departed for his Oakland writing desk in November of 1873. The transcontinental railroad, completed in 1869, now made travel from the East to the wonders of California far easier than in the days when Horace Greeley endured endless weeks in dusty stagecoaches across the West and then a bumpy mule ride that pulverized his rear end before delivering him, tired and cranky, to Yosemite Valley.

Visitation had reached 2,530 tourists for the summer season, five times the number of the early years, even though the final trails down to the Merced were still too steep and rugged for wagons. To accommodate the growing crowds, three hotels operated on the Valley floor, serviced by two carriages that had been assembled—one by Galen Clark, the second by James Mason Hutchings when he saw the profit in it—after their pieces were packed in by mules. The Cosmopolitan did a brisk business offering "brandy cocktails, eye-openers, corpse revivers, and other potent combinations" in its ornate saloon; hot baths in its five private, carpeted bathrooms, equipped with Turkish towels and bottles of cologne; a barbershop and bootblack; a gentleman's reading room; a laundry service; and two billiard tables (also packed in by mules). Room and board at the hotels generally ran $3.50, renting a horse cost $2.50, and hiring a guide was $5.00 per day. "Yosemite's not as bad as Niagara," one visitor said, "but money melts very fast."

Just above the Valley, Snow's Hotel sat near the base of Nevada Fall, at the end of a toll trail. And the

The brochure for the Cosmopolitan promised Yo-Semite
Cobblers and Bridal Veil Juleps as well as billiard tables, baths,
and a barbershop.

enterprising James McCauley had completed the Four Mile Trail to Glacier Point, where he, too, planned to open a hotel. His toll path to the dramatic overlook was so popular, it earned back his $3,500 investment and started paying a profit within two years. "Although it is far the steepest out of the valley, zigzagging back and forth on a sheer granite wall," the writer and activist Helen Hunt Jackson wrote, "one rides up it with little alarm or giddiness, and with such a sense of gratitude to the builder that the dollar's toll seems too small." In 1874, within a month

of each other, two wagon roads were finally completed into the Valley from the north—the Coulterville Road and then the Big Oak Flat Road—and regular stage service finally commenced. Both roads were greeted by gala celebrations that included grand processions of carriages, fireworks, marching bands, bonfires on the cliffs, and, not surprisingly, grandiose speeches by the master of ceremonies, James Mason

When the financially hapless Galen Clark sold Clark's Station, the new owner made improvements to the Mariposa Road and built the Wawona Hotel to handle the increased tourist traffic.

Hutchings, still firmly ensconced in the Valley he viewed as his own fiefdom, and happy that customers could now reach his expanding collection of hotels in relative comfort.

For Galen Clark, the completion of the two carriage roads from the north spelled financial doom. Traffic along the southern Mariposa Road dwindled. Clark's Station became insolvent and was turned over to its principal creditor, a savvy businessman with deep pockets. The new owner hired a crew of three hundred Chinese workers to build the Wawona Road to Inspiration Point and down to the Valley. Clark's Station became the Wawona Hotel, and business picked up again, though too late for the monetarily hapless Clark. At least part of Frederick Law Olmsted's plan had been realized: the Yosemite Grant was now much more accessible to the public. But Clark, its Guardian, was sixty years old and broke—still waiting in vain for the state legislature to pay him for all his work—and the larger question of whether the Grant was indeed a public trust remained unanswered, as long as Hutchings refused to acknowledge it. His claim still had the support of the state legislature and he made another run at Congress to ratify it. To generate public support, Hutchings toured the East, showing stereopticon lantern slides of the scenic wonders on an eighteen-foot square canvas, touting himself as a pioneer martyr fighting against the government to hold on to his family's "little homestead in Yosemite," and financing his lobbying junket by charging an admission of twenty-five cents (fifty cents for reserved seats) to crowds that in some

instances reached three thousand. In all, Hutchings gave a total of eighty-seven speeches in cities like Boston, New York, Philadelphia, and the real target of his promotional blitz: Washington, D.C. Once again, the House of Representatives backed Hutchings's and Lamon's claims of prior ownership; once again, the Senate wouldn't budge, but only on a close vote.

Meanwhile, the lawsuit trying to eject Hutchings moved forward. First, a California district court decided in his favor, but the state's supreme court overturned it and ruled for the commissioners. Hutchings appealed to the United States Supreme Court. Here the arc of history reached an inflection point. In *Hutchings v. Low*, the nation's highest court was asked, in essence, whether it was constitutional for Congress to reserve land from development for national public parks; or whether, as the decision stated, the act of "mere settlement" could "deprive Congress of the power to reserve such lands from sale for public uses of the United States."

The court ruled in the public's favor and against Hutchings, noting first that Congress had not ratified California's attempt to grant Hutchings private rights within the Grant, but then going out of its way to speak as forcefully as possible. "It is not believed," the justices intoned, "that Congress will ever sanction such a perversion of the trust solemnly accepted by the State." In his desire to further his own narrow interests, Hutchings had unintentionally provided the still-nascent park idea with the imprimatur of the nation's highest court. A clear precedent had been set: a national park is a solemn trust; privatizing it constitutes a perversion. Thank you, James Mason Hutchings.

Perversion or not, Hutchings wasn't giving up. For two years he refused to vacate his property, and in 1874 he persuaded his friends in Sacramento to appropriate sixty thousand dollars to buy out all the claims in the Valley. Naturally, he collected the biggest share—twenty-four thousand dollars—but when Clark and the commission told him the only way he could continue running his business was to fill out a written application for a lease, Hutchings contemptuously refused, threatened to sue anyone who applied in his stead, and defiantly opened for the 1875 season. In May the Mariposa County sheriff showed up with legal orders and formally evicted him.

Even that wasn't enough. Out of sympathy for the family, the kind-hearted Clark gave in to Hutchings's pleas to let him store some personal belongings in an empty building. Next thing Clark knew, Hutchings was running a hotel in it, having moved his Wells Fargo office, his telegraph equipment, and the Valley's post office to the new location. Clark asked him to leave once more. Hutchings refused, "using language," one commissioner noted, "too profane to repeat." The *Mariposa Gazette* was kinder and more discreet: "In the classical language of our friend, he promises to remain in his new abode until hell freezes over, and the devil can take a trip to Yosemite on the ice." There Hutchings remained through the rest of the season. In the fall, the sheriff escorted him out of the Valley. Back in San Francisco, Hutchings continued in the tourist business, leading groups to

Yosemite in the summer, lecturing across California, selling small guidebooks for sixty cents each while he worked on a heftier book, publishing a seed catalog that offered, among other things, a pound of sequoia seeds for twelve dollars—and plotting to return permanently to the park from which he had been so unceremoniously expelled.

◄○►

THE CEASELESS PROBLEMS with Hutchings took a toll on Galen Clark's health. The *Mariposa Gazette* reported he was struck with "partial paralysis on the side of his head and face" for a while, and on the big day when the Wawona Road brought in the first stagecoach from what had once been Clark's longtime home and station, he was not among the speakers. The increased visitation also added to his stress as Guardian of the Yosemite Grant. Tourists besieged him with questions, complained to him about high prices and unsatisfactory meals and rude guides and the disappointing absence of water in Yosemite Falls in the dry season. Hotelkeepers griped about unpaid bills and damages from unruly guests and that the Cosmopolitan's bar was unfairly cutting into their own liquor sales.

Troubles continued to haunt Clark's personal life, as well. His son Alonzo had moved west, rejoining him after a seventeen-year separation, and tried to help out with running Clark's Station, but Alonzo's health was even more frail than his father's. He died in 1873 from either consumption or congestive heart failure at the age of twenty-six. A year

The improved roads from Coulterville and Wawona (above)
meant carriages could now bring visitors all the way to the Valley.

later, after a quarter century as a widower, Clark
came back from a trip to San Francisco with a new
wife. The bride was twenty years younger than
Clark—a large, swarthy woman with a thick accent,
named Isabella Pearce but also known as Madame
Solemna, a fortune-teller. The suspicion in Yosemite
Valley abounded that she had married the Guardian
for his money—a suspicion that hardened when she
left him a few years later, once it became unmistak-
ably clear that making money was not one of Galen
Clark's skills.

He was living in a small cabin in the Valley
now, still consumed with his many duties. In 1878

the commissioners directed him to fence in a hundred
acres of Lamon's former property, so a public camp-
ground could be provided to visitors who didn't want
to stay in the hotels. Two bridges were replaced, plus
a new one constructed across a narrow stretch of the
Merced near El Capitan, where the glacial moraine
had deposited many boulders, creating something of
a natural dam that backed up water in the springtime, flooding many of the meadows. This made land
travel difficult at times and provided a rich breeding
ground for mosquitoes. Clark's solution was dramatically simple (and would probably not be approved
today): he brought in black powder and blasted out
the boulders to create a freer-flowing river.

He wrote articles for the *California Farmer* about
the legislature's consistent refusal to appropriate the

money the park needed for its improvements, and how the proliferation of toll roads went against the grain of a "free park for the world." In 1879 when the California Sunday School Association began a fundraising effort to build a chapel in the Valley, Clark took the unpopular (and ultimately unsuccessful) stance against it:

> It seems to *me* almost like sacrilege to build a church within the portals of this the grandest of all God's temples. It is like building a toy church within the walls of St. Peter's cathedral in Rome.
>
> But it will clearly show the contrast between the frail and puny works of man, as compared with the mighty grandeur and magnificence of the works of God, and I hope it will do good.

Publicly decrying the legislature's failures and opposing an association of Sunday schools was not a good career move for a state employee. In 1879 California adopted a new constitution, and one of its provisions limited the tenure of state officials. The result was an entirely new board of commissioners for the Yosemite Grant, whose first order of business was to dump Clark after fourteen years of dedicated service. In selecting a new Guardian, they chose a man who had been patiently working behind the scenes for political revenge, predicting "hope of a new and glorious day dawning in Yosemite." They chose the man who had done his utmost for more than a decade to prevent the Grant from becoming what Frederick Law Olmsted had envisioned. They chose, of all people, the indefatigable James Mason Hutchings.

Galen Clark's public criticism of building the Yosemite Valley chapel—"almost like sacrilege," he said—helped cost him his job as Guardian.

Hutchings quickly moved back into his old cabin and issued a report denigrating the work of his nemesis and predecessor, Galen Clark. "It is with more than passing regret," he wrote, his pen dripping with gall, "I have to mention that on careful examination of the Valley, its condition forcibly convinces me that much earnest and serviceable work has to be done to redeem it from the apparent neglect into which it has fallen, and make it popular with the public."

It's difficult not to be hard on Hutchings, considering him through the lens of 150 years of history. He comes down to us as a shameless self-promoter whose first instincts were mercenary, a businessman who may have loved Yosemite but whose combination of ego and commercial ambition blinded him to a larger good. But he was actually fairly representative of his era, a little more vain and bombastic than many businessmen perhaps—the P. T. Barnum of Yosemite—but very much in sync with the prevailing ethics of the day, whether it was openly manipulating the legislature for his personal interests or viewing the natural world as a commodity to be exploited without much thought of the consequences, and doing so without any apology or artful dodging. Today we look back at him through the filter of a culture in which conservation has become part of the shared American creed, even if significant portions of society still pay only lip service to it. (His philosophical descendants are very much still with us; they just have learned to be more circumspect about it.) In Hutchings's time, "conservation" wasn't even a word in common use, let alone a movement, even less an accepted part of society's mainstream beliefs. In the context of his own time, Hutchings becomes much less of a villain (many were much worse) and more of an archetype.

His energy and drive, his sheer refusal to be defeated, were undeniable. The large crowds he attracted on his speaking tour attest to the power of his oratory, or at least the intense interest people in the East had for hearing more about Yosemite. He was a prolific writer, though nowhere near John Muir on the eloquence scale. And his zeal for Yosemite burned so brightly that guests at his hotel complained about his propensity to launch into lectures about the scenery while at the same time filling their coffee cups with cold water at breakfast or failing to provide them with knives and forks at dinner. "Guests would be better served," one patron wrote, "if the proprietor paid less attention to describing the beauties and more to providing comfortable beds and properly prepared meals."

Clark's replacement was none other than James Mason Hutchings, who had been evicted only a few years earlier.

Hutchings also had his own share of personal travails. After years of unhappiness, his first wife, Elvira, had abandoned him and their children sometime in the late 1870s, and the couple divorced. (Feeling isolated and depressed in Yosemite Valley, Elvira had developed a deep affection toward Muir during their long walks and conversations; whether the relationship was anything more than that—most historians say it was close but platonic—Hutchings felt aggrieved about it.) His house in San Francisco had burned down in 1880, taking his papers and extensive collection of photographs with it. Shortly after returning to Yosemite, his spirited eighteen-year-old daughter Florence (called Floy), who had been the first white child born in the Valley and was beloved by everyone, was killed in a freak accident climbing to Glacier Point. Six weeks later, his second wife died from a lung hemorrhage.

Still, the facts are what they are, and one of the most telling facts about James Mason Hutchings is how repeatedly he quarreled with John Muir and Galen Clark over the fate of Yosemite. Forced to take sides in that fight, the choice isn't difficult. With his connections, Hutchings finally squeezed some money out of the state legislature to purchase the toll roads and toll trails within the Grant and make them free to the public. But he couldn't change his personality. He soon began bickering with the new

One of the most telling facts about Hutchings is how repeatedly he quarreled with Clark and Muir.

commissioners, and in 1884 they fired him after only three years on the job.

Hutchings's successor lasted only two years, during which he permitted overgrazing in the meadows. The next man, also a political appointee, was equally incompetent and drew so much criticism that the state senate launched an investigation of the commission's oversight. When he was fired in 1889, a new Guardian was needed to repair the commission's tattered image. They found such a person already in the Valley. He had recently been making his living driving a "tourist coach," a three-seated carriage, for people who wanted to learn about the sites as they were taken from one to the other. He had also been appointed postmaster of the Valley. Now, even though he was seventy-five, he would be Guardian: Galen Clark was back where he belonged.

◄O►

The man of science, the naturalist, too often loses sight of the essential oneness of all living beings in seeking to classify them in kingdoms, orders [and] species . . . while the eye of the Poet, the Seer, never closes on the kinship of all God's creatures, and his heart ever beats in sympathy with great and small alike as "earth-born companions and fellow mortals" equally dependent on Heaven's eternal love.

—John Muir

BACK IN 1875, in the midst of all the political and administrative turmoil within the Grant, a new tourist attraction was added to Yosemite's list. George C. Anderson, a powerfully built laborer and guide, announced he had not only climbed Half Dome, but had made it accessible to others who wanted to share the dramatic view. People had been trying to reach the 8,836-foot summit for sixteen years. Hutchings had tried in 1859 but found the round back shoulder of the dome to be "a great smooth mountain . . . at an angle of about 40 degrees [actually 46 degrees], its surface overlaid and overlapped, so to speak, with vast circular granite shingles, about eighteen inches in thickness. There was not a place to set a secure foot upon, or a point that we could clutch with our fingers." None other than Josiah D. Whitney, the state geologist, had declared in 1868 that Half Dome "never has been, and never will be trodden by human foot"—a confident prediction proven just as wrong as Whitney's equally confident contention that the monolith's flat face had been created by a cataclysmic collapse.

Anderson scaled the final, treacherous 975 feet of Half Dome by patiently drilling a hole in the rock face, then pounding in an iron eye bolt, pulling himself up to stand on it, then reaching up to repeat the process until he made it to the top. Then he threaded a heavy, braided rope through the rings (the prototype for today's steel cables). News of his achievement was electrifying. In less than a week, six men and one woman used Anderson's ropeway for the panoramic view atop Tis-se'-yak and had the bragging rights for

saying they had done it. Galen Clark, age sixty-one at the time, was one of them. John Muir hurried from Oakland to Yosemite in November to become the ninth person. When he reached the top, with the Valley below him encased in a low cloud cover and the sun behind him, he was rewarded for his effort by the rare phenomenon called the "Brocken spectre" and its halo-like glory. Muir was enthralled:

> My shadow, clearly outlined, about half a mile long, lay upon this glorious white surface with startling effect. I walked back and forth, waved my arms and struck all sorts of attitudes, to see every slightest movement enormously exaggerated.
>
> A grander surface and a grander standpoint . . . could hardly have been found in all the Sierra.

That long shadow neatly symbolized what had become of Muir since embarking on a writing career. Even though he had given up permanent residence in the Valley, he had become more closely associated with Yosemite in the public's mind—and much better known—than either Hutchings or Clark. Even though he still made periodic visits to the Valley and the high country, and even though his central message was the one forged by the "unconditional surrender" to Nature he had experienced in Yosemite, his gaze now extended to larger vistas and his voice now reached larger audiences.

By the late 1880s Muir had published eighteen articles for *The Overland Monthly* and nearly eighty for the San Francisco *Evening Bulletin*. Many of them were about Yosemite, but the *Evening Bulletin* also used Muir as a roving correspondent,

dispatching him to send back his impressions from the Owens Valley and Lake Tahoe, from Nevada, Utah, and then Alaska Territory, where the scientist-turned-travel writer thrilled to spend time in the previously little-known Glacier Bay. There a river of ice met the ocean and Muir was once more in ecstasy. His reports—the first descriptions of Glacier Bay to reach the nation—proved so popular that the *Evening Bulletin*'s circulation increased, copies were reprinted all over the country, and a steamship company was soon running cruises to places it called "Muir Inlet" and "Muir Glacier," in the belief that his name alone would attract paying customers.

Harper's New Monthly Magazine commissioned four stories on glaciers, then *Scribner's Monthly* signed him up for ten outdoor essays, which ranged from the majesty of Yosemite and the Sierra Nevada to the joy of quietly observing everything from the Douglas squirrel to his beloved water ouzel. Laboring over a pen and paper was tedious and confining work for the mountaineer. Writing, he said, is "like the life of a glacier, one eternal grind." But Muir was steadily reaching a national readership, preaching his gospel of Nature, and his reputation was growing with each sermon. (He also was in demand as a lecturer and at one point gave two speeches on glaciation in the Yosemite chapel—a fitting venue for someone who wrote that any man who believes in neither God nor glaciers is "the worst of all unbelievers.")

Opposite: George Anderson, who first ascended Half Dome and made it accessible to others, surveys the Valley at his feet.

In 1880 Muir married Louie Wanda Strentzel and settled down with her on her parents' prosperous agricultural estate near Martinez, California. Two daughters quickly followed. Muir found himself in charge of his in-laws' three thousand acres of orchards, growing cherries, Tokay grapes, and Bartlett pears. He threw himself into the work, improving the farm's productivity and amassing wealth for the first time, but also making only one trip to Yosemite in the course of eight years. His health seemed to suffer from his separation from the mountains. "Nerve-shaken and lean as a crow—loaded with care, work and worry," he wrote his brother. "I am losing precious days," he complained to a friend. "I am degenerating into a machine for making money. I am learning nothing in this trivial world of men. I must break away and get out into the mountains to learn the news."

Muir's wife recognized his need to reconnect with the wilderness. In 1885, when he was called back to Wisconsin to visit his ailing parents, she insisted that he make a one-week stop in the nation's second attempt at preserving a large landscape: Yellowstone National Park, which Congress had created thirteen years earlier, in 1872. The sequence of events in that creation had closely followed the pattern set by the Yosemite Grant. A magnificent place (in this case the headwaters of the Yellowstone River, a geological wonderland that includes the greatest collection of geysers in the world) came to the nation's attention through written reports, but most vividly through the work of artists (specifically the

Above: John Muir and his wife and their daughters at their home near Martinez

Opposite: When Muir wrote his wife, Louie, from Yellowstone in 1885, it was still the world's only national park.

paintings of Thomas Moran and the photographs of William Henry Jackson). A representative of a major company (the Northern Pacific Railroad), seeing the possibility of increased business from a spectacular tourist attraction, suggested: "Let Congress pass a bill reserving the Great Geyser Basin as a public park forever—just as it has reserved that far inferior wonder the Yosemite valley and big trees."

In Congress, supporters of the bill made the same argument for setting Yellowstone aside that Senator John Conness had made for Yosemite in 1864: it was "worthless" as farming land and seemingly without any mineral wealth; its value as a unique scenic icon could be ruined, like Niagara, if too many people staked individual claims there. In the Senate, to quell any lingering resistance to removing public land from development, the bill's sponsor specifically noted that a precedent for this sort of thing had

already been set with the Yosemite Grant, and added that the Supreme Court had upheld it as constitutional. In the House, the other principal sponsor also stressed the similarity with Yosemite, except for one difference: Yellowstone, he pointed out, was in Wyoming *Territory*. There was no state to take over management of it; therefore this proposed park would have to be a federal responsibility. And so, though modeled in every respect on the Yosemite Grant eight years earlier, Yellowstone—the first transplant from Yosemite's seed—became the world's first *national* park. It was a distinction arising more out of happenstance than intention—a seemingly slight mutation of the original Yosemite species—but in time it would prove to be of the utmost significance, a turning point in the evolution of the park idea.

John Muir arrived at the young national park via the Northern Pacific, tired and sicker than he'd been since his bout of malaria in Florida. His stomach seemed to mimic the hot springs and mud pots and geysers. When Old Faithful erupted, he wrote, "my organ began spouting vast quantities of hot acid water in close accord." The weather was cold and wet. In his weakened state, he fell from his horse and

suffered an injury. But he completed a 150-mile tour through the park, seeing "Nature at work as chemist or cook . . . making the most beautiful mud in the world," and encouraging others to "take a look into . . . the grand geological library of the park, and see how God makes history." His health hadn't improved, but at least he had visited "the Wonderland" and seen another way for land to be protected.

Three years later, in 1888, still concerned about her husband's weakened condition, Louie persuaded Muir to return to the mountains again. He should give up farm work, she told him—the family could live comfortably enough leasing the estate he had made so efficient and profitable—and focus instead on his true calling as Nature's apostle. He went first to Lake Tahoe and Mount Shasta in northern California, then to the forests of Oregon and Washington, all the while noticing the wholesale destruction now being wrought by the lumber interests on the public domain. Muir thought a few of the places should be saved as national parks before it was too late, so that some trees, at least, "might be spared to the world, not as dead lumber, but as living trees." And looking to the more distant future, he contemplated the legacy that park creators and park protectors might leave to posterity:

> Happy will be the men who, having the power and the love and the benevolent forecast to do this, will do it. They will not be forgotten. The trees and their lovers will sing their praises, and generations yet unborn will rise up and call them blessed.

Camping on the slopes of Mount Rainier in Washington State, "the most extravagantly beautiful of all the Alpine gardens I ever beheld," he felt some of his old energy return and impulsively joined a group of younger men to make the sixth recorded ascent of its more than fourteen-thousand-foot summit. "Did not mean to climb it," Muir wrote his wife, "but got excited and soon was on top." The climb had left him with "heart and limb exultant and free," and it deepened his appreciation of the profound impact of wilderness on human existence. "The mountains are fountains of men as well as of rivers, of glaciers, of

fertile soil," he wrote. "The great poets, philosophers, prophets, able men whose thoughts and deeds have moved the world, have come down from the mountains—mountain-dwellers who have grown strong there with the forest trees in Nature's workshops."

Back home in 1889 he was primed for action when Robert Underwood Johnson, the associate editor of *The Century*, a New York magazine with a million readers and substantial influence, arrived to ask Muir to write for the magazine. The two embarked for Yosemite, reaching the Valley the same month the drumbeat of complaints was embarrassing the commissioners enough to rehire Galen Clark as Guardian of the Yosemite Grant. Everywhere he looked, Muir was dismayed at what state management had done to the place he considered Nature's temple.

To attract business to the Big Oak Flat Road, promoters had carved a tunnel through the base of a giant sequoia in the Tuolumne Grove so tourists could drive their carriages through it. (James Mason Hutchings claimed credit for this publicity stunt and had a photograph taken of him going through the tunnel tree for his book *In the Heart of the Sierras*.) In response, the owners of the Wawona Hotel, along the competing road to the south, had sought permission from the commissioners to hack out their own tunnel through a sequoia in the Mariposa Grove, creating an even more popular attraction, where photographers made a good living taking pictures of tourists posing in front of it. (The Wawona Tunnel Tree eventually became the most photographed tree in the world; when winter snows blocked access to it in the upper

On the summit of Mount Rainier in 1888, Muir (sitting among his companions) felt "exultant and free" to be back in the mountains he loved.

Above: Hutchings (far right) claimed credit for the idea of carving a carriage tunnel through a giant sequoia on the Big Oak Flat Road. To compete, the owners of the Wawona Hotel did the same thing in the Mariposa Grove.

Opposite: Overhanging Rock on Glacier Point became a favorite spot for tourists to have their picture taken.

grove, the promoters cut a tunnel through the California Tree in the lower grove near the ever-popular Grizzly Giant, put the Wawona Tree sign in front of it, and guided happily unknowing tourists to it.)

At Glacier Point, 3,254 feet above the Valley, where Muir had once contemplated the view in reverent silence, Overhanging Rock had been turned into a platform for tourists to mug for the camera. Patrons at McCauley's Mountain House often spent idle moments dropping rocks tied in handkerchiefs over the edge, simply to watch them fall. James McCauley himself sometimes tossed a live chicken off the precipice. "With an ear-piercing cackle that gradually grew fainter as it fell," one person remembered, "the poor creature shot downward; now beating the air with ineffectual wings, and now frantically clawing at the very wind." To the shocked onlookers, McCauley would laugh and say: "Don't be alarmed about the chicken, ladies. She's used to it. She goes over that cliff every day during the season." He promised that the drop wouldn't injure the chicken, and sure enough, hours later they'd see it walking back up his Four Mile Trail. At night McCauley concocted an even more dramatic spectacle. His sons would collect donations to stage a "firefall"—a hugely popular event in which they built a giant bonfire on Glacier Point and then, at a signal from the crowds gathered below, pushed the glowing embers over the brink in a fiery cascade.

Muir was disgusted by a small dam built by a hotel owner to reroute the Liberty Cap Cascades toward Nevada Fall. This, Muir noted, was "Amer-

ican enterprise with a vengeance. Perhaps we may yet hear of an appropriation to whitewash the face of El Capitan or correct the curves of the Dome." In the Valley itself there were plans to illuminate the waterfalls with colored lights. The meadows had been converted into plowed hayfields and fenced pastures—even a hog pen whose stink, Muir wrote, "has got into the pores of the rocks."

In all, the atmosphere more closely resembled a circus than a sanctuary, and Muir hastened from it to show Robert Underwood Johnson the high country that had transformed his life twenty years earlier. But here, too, much had changed. The forests and alpine meadows lay outside the Yosemite Grant and therefore enjoyed even less protection than the Valley. Sheep barons had found the prospect of free grass irresistible and turned their herds loose each summer, over-grazing to such an extent, Johnson wrote, that "Muir told me that they not only nibbled off everything in sight but that they succeeded in digging up the roots of most plants, so that nothing but bar-renness was left." Lumbermen also faced no restraints on this part of the public domain. The result was devastation.

Johnson urged Muir to put his passion and his growing reputation to work.

While they camped at Soda Springs in Tuolumne Meadows, Muir's mood alternated between anger and anguish as they talked. Johnson urged Muir to put his passion and his growing reputation to work. He proposed that Yosemite be made a national park, like Yellowstone. Johnson would organize the campaign, he promised, if Muir would provide two articles for *The Century*, using his unique voice to describe what was at stake and galvanize public opinion. In practi-cal political terms, the Yosemite Grant might have to be left under state control. (The two men discussed recruiting Frederick Law Olmsted to return and set things right in what Muir called "our grand 'Central Park' in the Sierra.") But at the very least, the high country desperately needed federal protection.

Muir wrote the two articles, which appeared in the late summer of 1890: "The Treasures of the Yosemite," an eloquent description of the Range of Light, and "Features of the Proposed Yosemite National Park," in which he even provided a map outlining his suggested boundaries. Johnson's lob-bying had already produced a bill before Congress

for a park of two hundred square miles; Muir's map called for a park seven times as large, embracing the headwaters of the entire Merced and Tuolumne River watersheds, including the Hetch Hetchy Valley.

At this point the Yosem-ite commissioners belatedly sprang into action. They had initially favored an enlarge-ment of the state-controlled Yosemite Grant into some of the high country, but with the commissioners still very much in charge of it. The notion of a huge federal park surround-ing their domain was unacceptable, as was a provi-sion calling for a federal investigation into whether the commission had fulfilled its duties. To fight the bill, Commissioner John P. Irish, editor of an Oak-land newspaper, resorted to slanderous name-calling. "Before he abandoned himself to profitable rhapsody and became a pseudo-naturalist," Irish wrote, Muir "figured among the squatters in the Yosemite" and had "cut and logged and sawed the trees of the Val-ley with as willing a hand as any lumberman." None of it was true, as Muir pointed out in his response: "I never cut down a single tree in the Yosemite, nor sawed a tree cut down by any other person there. Furthermore, I never held, or tried to hold, any sort of claim in the valley, or sold a foot of lumber there or elsewhere." Bad blood had been spilled out in the

Opposite: No spectacle was more unnatural—or more popu-lar—than the nightly "firefall" of burning embers pushed off Glacier Point.

The Century used this illustration (showing Tuolumne Meadows
and Mount Dana and Mount Gibbs) to accompany Muir's call for
a national park in Yosemite's high country.

open, but the commission's counteroffensive proved as ineffectual as its management of the Valley.

Johnson had solicited a supportive letter from Olmsted and circulated it to the right people. He initiated public petitions that flooded Congress, and enlisted the considerable political muscle of the Southern Pacific Railroad, which saw protection of the Sierra watersheds as beneficial to its farming clients in the Central Valley and a new park in California as good for passenger traffic. The combined pressure resulted in Muir's boundaries being substituted for the smaller plan, and the revised bill, encompassing 932,000 acres under federal protection, sailed through both houses of Congress on September 30, 1890. President Benjamin Harrison signed it into law on October 1. Included in the bill were two other provisions that pleased Muir and Johnson: one enlarged a small park that had been created a week earlier to protect some sequoias farther south, to be called Sequoia National Park; the other created an even tinier park, General Grant, with one grove of big trees.

There were now four national parks. The seed that had been planted in the Yosemite Grant of 1864 had spread and evolved again. It had drifted to the Rocky Mountains and sprouted as Yellowstone National Park and then, with Muir's help, drifted back in its new form to its original home in the Sierra Nevada, finding fertile soil at Sequoia and General Grant National Parks. The other new park surrounded the seedbed of the original idea. Yosemite National Park, nearly fifteen-hundred square miles, stretched from the Valley's edge east to the crest of the Range of Light and north to embrace the entire Hetch Hetchy Valley, which Muir considered "a grand landscape garden, one of Nature's rarest and most precious mountain temples." At the massive new national park's center, however, was the Yosemite Valley, and to its side was the Mariposa Grove, both still under state control—a park within a park. The next fight would be to unite them as one park. A *national* park.

6

UNCLE SAM'S SOLDIERS

The very first reservation that ever was made in this world . . . contained only one tree—the smallest reservation that ever was made. Yet, no sooner was it made than it was attacked by everybody in the world—the devil, one woman and one man.

This has been the history of every reservation that has been made since that time; that is, as soon as a reservation is once created then the thieves and the devil and his relations come forward to attack it.

—JOHN MUIR

BY 1890 THE AMERICAN EXPERIMENT in preserving large natural landscapes for the benefit of everyone was still an uncertain endeavor. Yes, four national parks now existed, but they were mere seedlings. What form they might take, whether they would even survive to the sapling stage, let alone maturity, was still an open question. What, exactly, *was* a national park? How were visitors expected to experience it? What, after all, was the park preserving—scenery, wildlife, flora, watersheds, tranquility? And who was responsible for their protection? No one knew for sure. It was all being worked out on the fly, in the tensions and tug of war that define the evolution of all American ideas.

In Yellowstone the early years of testing the national model had been marked by confusion and chaos. Tourists thought nothing of carving their names into the rock features. They tossed logs into geyser openings to see if the next discharge would spit them back up, or dumped in laundry soap on the belief that it would induce an eruption. Hunters routinely shot the elk and bison with abandon. There was no one to stop them.

The Northern Pacific Railway, which had pushed for the park's creation and brought tourists to the park's entrance on its trains, had quickly exerted a monopoly within Yellowstone, controlling the hotels, the stagecoaches, the tents, the food, the guides. "By God," one person complained, "they're fixing that thing so that if you want to take a whiff of a park breeze, you will have to pay for the privilege of turning your nose in that direction." At one point, in what came to be called "the Park Grab," the company secretly began negotiations with the

Secretary of the Interior to be granted seven parcels of land, each 640 acres, surrounding the prime attractions. At another time the railroad nearly got approval to extend its lines through the park, rather than to its borders. A string of incompetent, politically appointed superintendents included one who removed an entire geyser cone for display in the Smithsonian and proposed that Liberty Cap, a distinctive rock formation, be outfitted with plumbing so it could project a steady column of water. Another superintendent was caught filing preliminary land claims at choice spots, in hopes the northern part of the park would be reopened for settlement.

Army men in formation at Liberty Cap in Yellowstone National Park

Five Buffalo Soldiers, members of the Twenty-Fourth Mounted Infantry, on patrol in Yosemite

Congress considered proposals to follow the Yosemite model and turn Yellowstone over to Wyoming, once the territory became a state, or to abandon the notion of a national park altogether. "I do not understand myself what the necessity is for the Government entering into the show business in Yellowstone National Park," Senator John Ingalls of Kansas told his colleagues. "I should be very glad myself to see [it] surveyed and sold, leaving it to private enterprise. . . . The best thing that the Government could do with the Yellowstone National Park is to survey it and sell it as other public lands are sold."

An unlikely coalition of prominent citizens rose up to resist all these efforts. Led by George Bird Grinnell, publisher of *Forest and Stream*, who called Yellowstone "the people's park," it included a handful of senators and congressmen; General Phil Sheridan, who believed the park's boundaries should be doubled in size to provide greater protection to the elk's and bison's migration patterns; and a rising young New York City politician named Theodore

Roosevelt. In 1886, when the congressional dead-lock resulted in the park's appropriation being eliminated, Yellowstone's superintendent and his assistants walked off their jobs. Sheridan sent Troop M of the United States Cavalry to the rescue, and the army found itself as the park's caretaker—a supposedly "stopgap" measure that would last for three decades.

With the creation of Sequoia, General Grant, and Yosemite National Parks, the cavalry took charge of these parks as well. Each spring, troops stationed at the Presidio in San Francisco would the make the two-week, 250-mile ride to the Sierra Nevada and patrol the three parks during the summer season. Some of them were Buffalo Soldiers, the celebrated African American troopers who had made a name for themselves in the Indian wars. (Most of the Buffalo Soldier units were commanded by white officers, but at Sequoia National Park, Captain Charles Young, born into slavery in Kentucky, became the first black man to be put in charge of a national park; the second would not be named until 1970.) The soldiers blazed trails in the high country, extinguished fires, kept their eye out for poachers, and did their best to put an end to cattle and sheep grazing in the alpine meadows.

Like their counterparts in Yellowstone, they operated in a legal no-man's land, because the legislation creating the parks had not provided anyone with clear authority to arrest and prosecute violators of park regulations. The most they could do was expel an offender. Yosemite's first acting superintendent, Captain A. E. "Jug" Wood, initially tried bluff-

Captain A. E. "Jug" Wood

ing. "The Yosemite Park is to be a Park throughout all time—it is not a temporary arrangement," he proclaimed in a newspaper announcement addressed to the region's cattlemen and sheep owners. "It would be better if the citizens living near the Park would make arrangements to conform to the new conditions of things, thus avoiding the consequence of a violation of the law."

That bluff didn't work. The first June, troopers reported nearly one-hundred-thousand sheep approaching the park's meadows from the south and west. Wood had four trespassing sheepherders arrested and brought to his headquarters at Wawona, "all for the effect." But the United States Attorney in San Francisco made a spectacle out of reprimanding Wood for exceeding his statutory jurisdiction, telling the newspapers "no criminal action could lie under the law." Now everyone knew the army was a paper tiger.

Captain Wood didn't give up. He improvised and switched tactics. He directed his troopers to follow the letter of the law: they would escort offending sheepherders to the park's boundary—but the ejection would be "a march consuming four or five days" to one side of Yosemite, while their herd would be released on the opposite side, many miles away. This proved more effective than a monetary fine ever could have. The illicit grazing came to an end, and the meadows revived. Likewise the poaching was stopped, and wild game staged a comeback, when Wood had his men confiscate visitors' firearms at park entrances and politely return them when the tourists left. At the same time, in the spirit of Frederick Law Olmsted, Wood said that everything he did was on behalf of the citizens who were the park's real owners: "I have tried, with some success, to impress the public mind with the fact that this Park was set apart, by the Congress, for the purpose of preserving the objects of wonder which nature has scattered with such a prodigal hand, within the limits of this Reservation, & that all, without distinction, are cordially invited to come & visit these wonderful creations, provided they observe the rules."

Like everyone else, Wood and his successors were feeling their way forward, groping really, relying on their own judgment to determine what was appropriate and what was not in a national park. The high-country rivers and lakes—above the tremen-

dous waterfalls of Yosemite Valley—were devoid of fish. Working with California's fish commissioners, Wood sent his patrols out with twenty-five thousand rainbow trout fingerlings to artificially stock the lakes, as if correcting one of Nature's oversights. The next year he introduced a nonnative species, twenty thousand New England brook trout, into the park. It was hugely popular with sportsmen—"The park is becoming probably the finest fishing grounds in the world," one army official boasted—but by another perspective that would evolve two generations later, it was an unnecessary and artificial alteration of a fully evolved ecosystem.

Because the military made a practice of rotating commanders every two or three years, and in the absence of established and well-thought-out policies, rules sometimes flipped back and forth with each changing of the guard. Concerns arose about all the private landholdings within Yosemite's new boundaries (ranches, timber claims, and even mining areas, totaling more than sixty-five thousand acres), which created an administrative nightmare in policing the park. Wood's recommended solution was redrawing the map, shrinking the park to "the only portion of the country that furnishes a reason for a national park," by which he meant the watershed headwaters and the best scenery. A later commander, worrying about the effect on wildlife if the lower parts of the park were excised, argued for the opposite solution: that the government should keep the boundaries intact and purchase all the private lands within them.

While Wood did everything in his power to suppress fires, believing (like John Muir, Galen Clark, and Robert Underwood Johnson) that all fires were mortal threats to the forest and should be extinguished as quickly as possible, Wood's successor, Captain George G. H. Gale, believed (as scientists do today) that regular fires were part of the natural cycle in the Sierra. A small fire across the forest floor every few years, he wrote, "burns easily with little heat, and does practically little damage. This fire also destroys, or partially destroys, the fallen timber which it touches, and leaves the ground ready

Robert Underwood Johnson

for the next year's growth . . . and it is not thought that the slight heat of the annual fires will appreciably affect the growth or life of well-grown trees." But, he continued:

> If the year's droppings are allowed to accumulate, they will increase until the resulting heat, when they do burn, will destroy everything before it [and] convert the forest into a roaring furnace.
>
> Examination of this subject leads me to believe that the absolute prevention of fires in these mountains will eventually lead to disastrous results.

The prevailing orthodoxy of Muir and the preservationists of the time ultimately won out, resulting in policies that tried to keep fires at bay—policies now seen as wrongheaded, for all the reasons Captain Gale enunciated. And the prevailing politics of the time ultimately meant that the dream of Muir and the preservationists to keep Yosemite's boundaries intact would be thwarted. In 1905, Congress would eliminate 542 square miles from the original park, mostly the sugar pine forests on the west and some mining and grazing districts to the southeast and southwest; meanwhile, it added 113 square miles of high mountain land by extending the northern boundary.

Like so much else in the development of the national park idea, the army's presence had been more the result of haphazard necessity than of farsighted vision, and its oversight was marked by fits and starts in its execution. But the officers and troopers had instilled a sense of nascent professionalism that marked the beginning of a new standard in park administration. No one ever accused the men in uniform of promoting their own interests over the interests of the parks under their care.

—◦—

In pleasing contrast to the noisy, ever-changing management or mismanagement, of blustering, blundering, plundering, money-making vote-sellers who receive their places from boss politicians as purchased goods, the soldiers do their duty so quietly that the traveler is scarcely aware of their presence.

[T]he soldiers have kept the sheepmen and sheep out of the park, and the grasses and blue gentians . . . are again blooming in all their wild glory. They found it a desert as far as underbrush, grass and flowers were concerned, but in two years the skin of the mountains is healthy again.

Blessings on Uncle Sam's soldiers. They have done the job well, and every pine tree is waving its arm for joy.

—John Muir

Despite his occasional differences of opinion with various commanders, and pacifist though he was, Muir remained steadfast in his belief that the army provided the best protection for Yosemite, just as he grew more and more convinced that only the federal government could be entrusted with ensuring its future. His association with Robert Underwood Johnson of *The Century* had exposed him to a national audience, and his interests in preserving Nature had become equally national. His feet and his heart might have still been on Half Dome, in the Range of Light, where he had found himself by sur-

rendering himself, but the shadow of his Brocken spectre now stretched across the continent, where it encountered a national movement that was already in motion and in need of an eloquent spokesman.

As the nineteenth century entered its closing decades, a growing number of Americans became alarmed at what the nation's headlong rush westward had done to the land and the natural world. Buffalo that once teemed over the Great Plains, numbering in the tens of millions, had been annihilated for their hides and reduced to a few hundred or even fewer. (Most them had found a final refuge in Yellowstone National Park; even there they were still being poached—killed solely for their heads, which were prized as trophies and commanded prices of one thousand dollars each in New York and London.) Great flocks of birds that had once darkened American skies had been devastated on an industrial scale by market hunters seeking to supply restaurants with meat, or women in big cities with exotic plumes for their hats. Timber syndicates that had laid waste to the woodlands of the upper Midwest were now mounting an assault on the public-domain forests of the mountain West. Mining had long since developed from a swarm of individual prospectors panning in streams to systems of powerful hydraulic hoses dismantling entire hillsides, and deep open pits beside smelters that belched arsenic-tinged smoke day and night.

Railroads now reached into every corner of the country. American Indians had been conquered and forced onto reservations. Towns had sprung up

Monument to the slaughter: thousands of bison skulls piled in Detroit, to be pulverized into bone black and fertilizer at the Michigan Carbon Works

in enough places that the director of the census of 1890 announced that, "There can hardly be said to be a frontier line." Seizing on that, a historian named Frederick Jackson Turner proclaimed: "And now, four centuries from the discovery of America, at the end of a hundred years of life under the Constitution, the frontier has gone, and with its going has closed the first period of American history."

In response to it all, some leaders stepped forward to say, "Stop." Publisher George Bird Grinnell, already involved in fighting "the Park Grab" in Yellowstone, rallied people against the heedless killing of birds by founding the Audubon Society. With his fellow New Yorker Theodore Roosevelt, he created the Boone and Crockett Club to lobby against the indiscriminate slaughter of the remaining big game animals. With an otherwise obscure congressman from Iowa, John F. Lacey, Grinnell managed to pass laws protecting migratory birds and putting enough teeth in Yellowstone's regulations that the bison were saved from extinction.

Muir's new friend, Robert Underwood Johnson, moved in the same circles. He had used his magazine and his influence to help create the high-country national park in Yosemite, and in 1891 he pushed for another one, farther south around Kings Canyon. To drum up support, Johnson paid Muir to revisit the area and write another article for *The Century*, "A Rival of the Yosemite," which described the region's

"It became clear that land conservation had become a legitimate and necessary part of American democracy."

beauty and the threats it was under (grizzly bears on the brink of extinction; trees of all species, including sequoias, being felled and fed to sawmills; and of course, sheep devouring any grass that could be found). Accompanying the article was a map proposing boundaries that added Kings Canyon to the new Sequoia National Park.

This time Congress wouldn't go along, but in a last-minute and little-understood addition to a different bill, on March 2, 1891, it ended up handing presidents the unilateral right to set aside forest reserves in the West. No one was entirely sure what the purpose of these reserves was—watershed protection, forest preservation, a momentary brake on the pell-mell advances of the timber syndicates—but President Benjamin Harrison soon flexed his new power. With strokes of his pen, he set aside forest reserves covering thirteen million acres, including the forests surrounding Yellowstone and the four million acres along the Sierra divide between Yosemite and Sequoia National Parks and surrounding Kings Canyon.

Another model for protecting large landscapes had been born—the national forest system—through a process that was just as messy, just as seemingly the result of happenstance, just as reliant on the earnest and sometimes behind-the-scenes efforts of individual citizens, and just as interconnected with Yosemite as the one that had created the national parks.

"Together," the eminent environmental historian Donald Worster has written, "the two kinds of federal conservation would eventually protect nearly three hundred million acres, reaching from the Everglades of Florida to the Brooks Range in northern Alaska. The birthing of those ideas occurred in the Yellowstone and Sierra regions during the infamous Gilded Age, but especially during the 1890–93 period when it became clear that land conservation had become a legitimate and necessary part of American democracy."

Johnson realized that Muir's passionate voice, as clear and musical as Yosemite Creek, was critical to the new movement. He urged Muir to form a citizen organization to advocate for the Sierra, much as Grinnell had done with the Audubon Society and the Boone and Crockett Club. Muir had demurred, but when some professors and students from the University of California approached him about joining a "Sierra Club," modeled after Portland's Alpine Club and Boston's Appalachian Mountain Club, Muir agreed to serve as its president, "hoping," he said, "that we will be able to do something for wildness and make the mountains glad."

But Muir belonged to a larger cause now, and Johnson lured him east to mingle with people of national influence, hoping Muir might inspire them with his gospel of Nature. He stopped in Chicago at the World's Columbian Exposition, whose grounds had been designed by Frederick Law Olmsted but whose message was the triumph of modern industry. In an alternative life, Muir might have been heralded there as one of the giants of American invention; now he was the champion of the forest in "a cosmopolitan's rat's nest." In New York he met with writers and scientists, including the famed naturalist John Burroughs. In Boston, Johnson introduced Muir to the historian-naturalist Francis Parkman and a bevy of Harvard notables; in Concord he visited the graves of Emerson and Thoreau, made a pilgrimage to Walden Pond, and was gladdened when Emerson's son told Muir how often his father had spoken of him. In Washington, D.C., he met with anyone Johnson thought might help their conservationist crusade.

When a national forestry commission was created in 1896, Muir was asked to travel with its members on their inspection tour of the West. He made friends with a young forester named Gifford Pinchot, who would later become the first head of the National Forest Service. The two men eventually split over Pinchot's willingness to permit sheep grazing in forest reserves, and later they would become antagonists over the fate of Hetch Hetchy Valley, but both men represented an emerging activism aimed at preventing the wholesale destruction of the natural world—an activism that saw the federal government as the only institution powerful enough to do it. Pinchot was the ultimate insider and over time would prove himself to be an astute politician. Muir recognized the need for political compromise if it advanced the cause, but to the public who read his words in *The Century*, *Harper's Weekly*, the *Atlantic Monthly*, and the other magazines now clamoring for his articles, his was the voice crying out in the wilderness:

Even sequoias in General Grant National Park weren't safe in
1891. Loggers pose proudly on the stump of the newly felled
Mark Twain Tree. Slabs were displayed in New York and London,
just as they had been a generation earlier.

Any fool can destroy trees. They cannot run away; and if they could, they would still be destroyed—chased and hunted down as long as fun or a dollar could be got out of their bark hides. . . .

Through all the wonderful, eventful centuries since Christ's time—and long before that—God has cared for these trees, saved them from drought, disease, avalanches, and a thousand straining, leveling tempests and floods; but he cannot save them from fools—only Uncle Sam can do that.

◄○►

MEANWHILE, YOSEMITE VALLEY and the Mariposa Grove continued under state control. Galen Clark, now in his late seventies, was still the Guardian. And the indomitable James Mason Hutchings was still a constant source of irritation. When the high-country national park had been created, Hutchings (though he had supported expanding the state Grant, not federal control) sensed another opportunity and quickly sent a letter to the Secretary of Interior claiming that numerous people were "kindly and warmly interesting themselves in my behalf for the position of superintendent," adding that California Senator Leland Stanford supported him for the job. The letter was ignored, and the army was dispatched instead.

Hutchings turned his attention back to the Valley. Each spring he applied for a lease to summer in his old cabin; each year the state commission turned him down "for reasons," they wrote, "that will be obvious to any member of the Commission who will consult the records." As usual, Hutchings went to the legislature to override the decision and prevailed, but

other disputes prevented him from moving back in. He continued writing his guidebooks and leading tours, seeking always to keep his name linked with Yosemite's. In 1894, "filled with regret and indignation at the so-called 'management' there," he wrote a letter for *The San Francisco Examiner*:

> Vandalism the most pronounced, with neglect that is positively criminal, and an indifference to results that is appalling . . . I am grieved to say are unrestrainedly rampant in the marvelous Valley.
>
> When? O! When? will the Deliverer come? When will an indignant public rise to the situation, and, in the interests of the great State who has such a wonder within its boundary, wrest the whole and profitable heritage from the hands of its destroyers?

Most of Hutchings's criticism was aimed at the removal of some trees in the Valley, reflecting a common complaint against the commission whenever it tried to restore some of the vistas that had been present during the early days, when the Indians routinely kept the underbrush and saplings from clogging the meadow borders. On this issue, Muir and Robert Underwood Johnson were with Hutchings, but his attack seemed so histrionic and personal that Clark felt compelled to respond. Some of the trees that had been cut were dead already, he wrote, and he had used his discretion in having them turned to firewood:

> Nature's wonderful prolific power in reproducing and enlarging the area of young forest growth in Yosemite is most marvelous, and if left entirely unchecked, the valley in a few years, comparatively, would become a veiled tangled wilderness.

If Yosemite is to be maintained as a Park for public resort and recreation, a careful and judicious use of the axe and fire will be absolutely necessary.

Consider the source, Clark suggested: when Hutchings was running his hotel, "he had more trees cut than has ever been cut since by all the other residents who have lived in the valley," and his cattle and horse herds had grazed at large. If Yosemite needed a "Deliverer," his name wasn't James Mason Hutchings.

Clark had his own complaints about the way things were going. The state was finally providing him with a steady paycheck (and he was solvent for the first time in his life), but the legislature still didn't appropriate the funds that were sorely needed for proper maintenance and improvements. Politics entered into too many of the commission's decisions. And just like the troopers in the high country, the Valley's Guardian was legally powerless to enforce many of the Grant's regulations. Muir's public criticism that loose stock was destroying much of the meadows' vegetation, Clark admitted in an annual report, was "not wholly false," because while the commission had enacted a stringent rule against it, "there is no penalty affixed for its violation."

By 1897, at age eighty-three, with his hearing diminished and eyesight weakening—and more than forty years after he had been given only months to live—Clark announced his retirement as Guardian. The commission let him lease his cabin in the Valley for a dollar a year, and he occasionally hired himself and his carriage out to tourists for guided trips. He gave hikers walking sticks he had cut from dead branches and sold seeds from pinecones he had collected. "No sojourner in Yosemite Valley counted his visit complete, until he had shaken hands and chatted with Galen Clark," one newspaper reported. "In this gray-bearded, kindly old man, there lived a wonderful soul."

Years earlier, Clark had been granted a plot in the Valley's cemetery and had transplanted some sequoia seedlings from the Mariposa Grove to surround his future gravesite. He had dug a well and installed a hand pump to make it easier to water the trees, and he had added a large granite boulder upon which his name was chiseled, awaiting the time when the dates would be added. Now he spent part of each week carefully tending his gravesite trees and working on what would become three small books: about Yosemite, the Indians who had originally called it home, and the big trees Clark considered "a connecting link between the present and a prehistoric Botanical age."

But while Clark was slowing down, life in the Yosemite Grant was getting more hectic. With the arrival of the railroad to nearby Raymond in 1896, visitation had increased to more than four thousand a season. Proposals abounded for attracting even more visitors. Install a powerful searchlight on Glacier Point was one suggestion, "which would be novel and exceedingly attractive, [and] could be made to illuminate in different colors the Yosemite Falls, Vernal and Nevada Falls . . . and the various domes and cliffs

Opposite: An aging Galen Clark stands guard over the Valley from Glacier Point.

142

. . . with its various rainbow colors." Another scheme called for building a tramway from the Valley floor to Glacier Point (an idea that would resurface a number of times in the twentieth century). Still another recommended a system of reservoirs and sluiceways just above the Valley's rim that would store water during the spring runoff and then deliver it in late summer, so the famous waterfalls would flow during the entire tourist season.

The park's accommodations were in constant turmoil. The Stoneman House, a grand but shoddily built hotel owned by the state, burned down because of defective chimneys. The legislature declined the commission's request for sixty thousand dollars to replace it. After James McCauley closed his Mountain House at Glacier Point at the end of the 1897 season and went to his ranch outside the park, the commissioners summarily awarded his lease to someone else and ordered the Grant's new Guardian to break into the hotel and toss out all of McCauley's belongings, so the new lessee's furniture and supplies could be moved in. Hearing the news, McCauley returned to Glacier Point, broke in himself, threw out the new furnishings, moved his back in, and threatened to shoot his rival. A county sheriff was called in to remove him.

In 1899 two schoolteachers from Redwood City, David and Jennie Curry, began offering an alternative type of accommodation: a tent camp that was half as expensive as the four-dollar-a-night hotels and soon included a permanent dining room, restrooms, bathhouse, tennis and croquet courts, and

a nightly campfire that ended with the revival of the spectacular "firefall" from the edge of Glacier Point. Camp Curry's success, in turn, prompted the creation of Camp Yosemite, a similar collection of canvas sleeping tents with wooden floors installed near the site of Hutchings's old sawmill. Galen Clark, now in his eighties, was hired as the ceremonial host.

The first season of the twentieth century started with a publicity stunt. Oliver Lippincott arrived in a brand-new, ten-horsepower Locomobile, the first horseless carriage to enter the Valley. Lippincott's motive was to generate attention for the photography shop he ran in the Valley and to advertise for the Locomobile company. For several weeks he motored around Yosemite, creating a sensation, frightening the horses, and ultimately taking his car to Glacier Point, so it could pose like all tourists out on Overhanging Rock. There, Lippincott contemplated his achievement:

> As we sat out on that cliff, on the very top of the world, as it seemed, looking at the people and then at the gigantic mountains, I had a realizing sense of what a very small thing man is, but my respect for my race grew as I reflected upon the wonders it can accomplish, scaling such heights without visible effort and merely by the aid of a little gasoline, some steam and inventive genius.
>
> . . . But would not modern ideas and modern inventions, intruding into the heart of primeval nature, rob it of much of its charm?
>
> Yet there is only one Yosemite, I reasoned, now inaccessible to the majority of people, and if modern invention can bring it closer to the people the result must be beneficial.

A stagecoach delivers tourists to Camp Curry's tent camp.

Lippincott's reverie sounded a faint, somewhat inverted echo of Frederick Law Olmsted's original exhortation to the State of California back in 1865: by all means, make sure that Yosemite is accessible to the people, but remember that preservation of the scenery comes first. Lippincott simply seems to have had the priorities backward. The crucial question had never been (and still isn't) whether the park had been set aside for people to enjoy and use, or whether roads and accommodations and other amenities would be needed and some businesses would profit from it.

The critical issue—the challenge embedded in the first seed of the park idea—was remember-ing that Yosemite had been preserved for all people to enjoy, *for all time*. "This duty of preservation is the first," Olmsted had proclaimed thirty-five years earlier, "because the millions who are hereafter to benefit . . . have the largest interest in it, and the largest interest should be first and most strenuously guarded." That was the essential bargain inherent in this democratic experiment with the land Americans deemed special and even sacred.

The car that Oliver Lippincott drove to Gla-cier Point represented the starkest possible proof that Olmsted's prediction of "the millions" who would

THE *"Locomobile"* IN YOSEMITE PARK.

This view shows the absolute control of the *"Locomobile"* under all conditions. Mr. Oliver Lippincott, of Los Angeles, made an extended tour in the Yosemite and climbed to the tops of the highest mountains without difficulty or accident.

Catalogue and interesting printed matter furnished on application.

ADDRESS ALL COMMUNICATIONS TO

THE *"Locomobile"* COMPANY OF AMERICA,

No. 11 Broadway, New York City.

(and should) visit Yosemite had not been just a rhetorical flourish. The new century, with its new technology, was most assuredly going to bring visitors in those numbers. The question was whether the system set up in 1864 when the experiment began—state control—was the best way to meet that challenge. The answer was increasingly tilting toward "no."

The newer, federal model of protection—the Yellowstone model, which had gotten off to a shaky start but then quickly adapted when the cavalry arrived—was increasingly seen as a better path to follow, especially by the leaders of the emerging conservation movement, who considered the fate of America's public lands as a *national* issue that transcended the sometimes parochial politics of a single state. John Muir, their new national voice, had favored federal jurisdiction of the Valley and Mariposa Grove from the moment he and Robert Underwood Johnson had proposed the national park in Yosemite's high country. Nearly a decade later, Muir was even more convinced. "I have little hope for the Yosemite [Grant]," he told Johnson. "As long as the management is in the hands of eight politicians appointed by the ever-changing Governor of California, there is but little hope."

Now that he was no longer a state employee, Galen Clark had come to the same conclusion. He had initially opposed proposals to return the Grant to the federal government, instead recommending

Opposite: When Oliver Lippincott drove the first car to Yosemite in 1900, the Locomobile Company made the most of it.

that landscape architects and photographic artists draw up a master plan (another, truer echo of Olmsted) and that the commission be limited to three members chosen for their competence rather than their connections. Finally, discouraged by the string of inept guardians who succeeded him and by the state's consistent, crippling stinginess toward the Yosemite Grant, Clark publicly endorsed receding it to the federal government.

But many people in California, even those who were loudly critical of the commission's management, saw the recession issue as one of state prestige. Returning the great treasure they had been entrusted with would be the equivalent of an adoptive parent giving back a precocious child, not because the youngster was too hard to handle but because the adults were failures as parents. That was too much pride for some people, especially in state political circles, to swallow, and in 1897 they easily defeated a bill in the state legislature to return the Grant and make it part of Yosemite National Park.

No one had more of his own self-esteem wrapped up in Yosemite than James Mason Hutchings. He considered himself—and legitimately so—the man who had first placed the Valley and its waterfalls and its trees before the world's amazed eyes. He was, in fact, not only the first real tourist to visit Yosemite, but also the originator of Yosemite's tourist industry. Promoter par excellence, he was incapable of not reminding the world of his role. "It was," Hutchings wrote a newspaper in 1895 with

typical bravado, "my good fortune to start this scenic and financial ball rolling."

Distinguishing himself and his interests from those of Yosemite had never been a strong point for Hutchings. It was natural—and very human—for him to feel possessive about the Valley; equally natural and human to conclude that whatever was good for him was good for Yosemite. He had developed a deep passion for Yosemite that was only equaled

The last photo of James Mason Hutchings, with his wife on their way to the Valley on October 31, 1902

by his passion for making money out of Yosemite. He saw no contradiction in those two passions, and perhaps there wasn't one. But if not a contradiction, sometimes there was a tension, and in choices of consequence Hutchings seems to have regularly favored his second passion—his bottom line and his fame.

He was a businessman and publicist first and foremost, and at least some part of his attitude toward Yosemite was as a means to an end.

As Hutchings joined the chorus publicly criticizing the hapless Yosemite Grant commission in the late 1890s, it's often hard to separate the legitimacy of his arguments from his own tangled past relations with the state's overseers. In pursuit of his own happiness, he had taken them to court, ignored their injunctions, and routinely gone around them to his friends in the legislature. Ironically, "for reasons obvious to [anyone] who will consult the records," Hutchings himself probably constituted one of the most powerful arguments for moving control of Yosemite from Sacramento to Washington, D.C.

By 1902 he was running the Calaveras Big Tree Grove Hotel with his fourth wife, Emily, and regularly publishing small guidebooks. Maybe it wasn't quite Yosemite, but it still connected him with the "scenes of wonder and curiosity in California" he had been publicizing for so long. ("Mr. Hutchings has never been successful and never has quite failed," Muir confided to his friend Harry Randall, who like Muir had worked at Hutchings's sawmill. Such is change in California.)

In late fall of that year, at eighty-two, Hutchings decided to make one more camping trip to the Valley that had become such a significant part of his life nearly half a century earlier. Traveling on the Big Oak Flat Road on the afternoon of October 31, 1902, he stopped his buggy long enough so that he and his wife could have their photograph taken before making the final descent to the Valley. Emily looks prim and severe in the picture; Hutchings, his head tilted back so that his broad-brimmed hat doesn't shade his face and snow-white whiskers, exudes a sense of genial confidence. Not long afterward, they rounded a corner on the steep and rocky trail, and El Capitan, with the gaping mouth of Ah-wah-nee behind it, presented itself in view. Hutchings was enraptured once more. He stood in his wagon to drink it all in. "It is like heaven," he told his wife.

Suddenly something startled the horses and they took off. First Emily and then her husband were thrown from the carriage; she landed safely, but Hutchings hit some rocks headfirst and died in her arms soon afterward. A few days later, in the Big Tree Room of what had once been called the Hutchings House, the funeral service was held for the man the *Mariposa Gazette* eulogized as "the Father of Yosemite." He was buried next to his daughter and second wife in the Valley cemetery near Yosemite Falls—the waterfall he had read about in 1855 as being six times higher than Niagara's and couldn't resist coming to see for himself, then invited the world to do likewise. A giant slab of granite—so heavy a team of twelve horses was required to move it—marks the graves. Nearby is a second marker, a stone cross that Emily originally intended to commemorate Hutchings's death site near the scenic turnout. But the operators of the stage line persuaded her not to place the reminder of the fatal accident along the road to the Valley, knowing that her late husband would have understood why. They thought it would be bad publicity.

7

TO LAST
THROUGH THE
AGES

The tendency nowadays to wander in wilderness is delightful to see. Thousands of tired, nerve-shaken, over-civilized people are beginning to find out that going to the mountains is going home; that wildness is a necessity; and that mountain parks and reservations are useful not only as fountains of timber and irrigating rivers, but as fountains of life.

Even the scenery habit in its most artificial forms, mixed with spectacles, silliness, and kodaks; its devotees arrayed more gorgeously than scarlet tanagers, frightening the wild game with red umbrellas—even this is encouraging, and may well be regarded as a hopeful sign for the future.

—JOHN MUIR

THE PUBLICATION OF JOHN MUIR's second book, *Our National Parks*, in 1902 further solidified his position as the nation's guide to the natural world—a world that seemed under assault in a rapidly urbanizing and industrial country, yet still offered its healing powers to those who sought it out. "Walk away quietly in any direction and taste the freedom of the mountaineer," Muir urged his readers. "Climb the mountains and get their good tidings. Nature's peace will flow into you as sunshine flows into trees. The winds will blow their own freshness into you, and the storms their energy, while cares will drop off like autumn leaves."

There were now five national parks. Washington State's Mount Rainier, the first national park created from a national forest, had been added in 1899 with

John Muir (right) with fellow naturalist John Burroughs on the
Harriman Expedition to Alaska

Muir's encouragement, after a five-year campaign led by the National Geographic Society, scientific groups interested in studying glaciers and old volcanoes, the tourist-minded Chambers of Commerce of Tacoma and Seattle, and the Northern Pacific Railroad, which had pushed for the first national park in Yellowstone back in 1872. Muir understood the economic and scientific rationales for national parks, but he had his own reasons for advocating for this one. "If in the making of the West," he wrote, "Nature had what we call parks in mind—places for rest, inspiration, and prayers—this Rainier region must surely be one of them." Muir knew this from experience; his impulsive ascent of Mount Rainier in 1888 had reinvigorated his health and turned him from raising cherries and pears to propagandizing for wilderness.

Besides describing Yellowstone, Yosemite, General Grant, Sequoia, and Mount Rainier in loving detail, Muir's book called for more parks, especially at "the most tremendous cañon in the world," Arizona's Grand Canyon, "as unearthly in the color and grandeur and quantity of its architecture, as if you had found it after death, on some other star; so incomparably lovely and grand and supreme is it above all the other cañons in our fire-moulded, earthquake-shaken, rain-washed, wave-washed, river and glacier sculpted world." He sang the praises of Washington's Olympic and Cascade Mountains, the Lake McDonald region of Montana, California's Mount Shasta, and, of course, Alaska, "the most extensive, least spoiled, and most unspoilable of the gardens of the continent . . . Nature's own reservation, and every

lover of wildness will rejoice with me that by kindly frost it is so well defended." All but Mount Shasta would some day join the ranks of national parks.

Muir was no longer the self-described "unknown nobody" who had ambled across the Sierra Nevada in search of a calling, or the unemployed millwright who happened upon James Mason Hutchings at just the right moment, or the "mere sheepherder" and "ignoramus" challenging the theories of California's top geologist. John Muir was now famous and respected. Mountain peaks, canyons, and glaciers bore his name. Harvard University had bestowed him with an honorary degree, his first college diploma. The nation's biggest railroad magnate, Edward Harriman, had invited him to join an elaborate expedition to Alaska with a constellation of scientific stars. Charles Sprague Sargent, the eminent tree expert and director of the Arnold Arboretum, had dedicated a volume of his *The Silva of North America* to Muir. In the spring of 1903 the two friends were planning a botanizing trip across Europe and Russia, when Muir suddenly had a change of plans.

"An influential man from Washington wants to make a trip into the Sierra with me," he wrote Sargent, apologetically postponing their trip, "and I might be able to do some forest good in talking freely around the campfire." The "influential man" was the President of the United States, Theodore Roosevelt, on his way to California as part of an unprecedented national tour: fourteen thousand miles, twenty-five states, one hundred and fifty towns and cities, and more than two hundred speeches in the space of eight weeks. But in the midst of it, before heading back to the White House from the Pacific, Roosevelt's biggest wish was to spend some time in Yosemite with the man who had written so passionately about it. "I do not want anyone with me but you," the president had written, "and I want to drop politics absolutely for four days and just be out in the open with you." Muir's trip around the world could wait. He quickly accepted and went out to buy a new woolen suit before joining the presidential entourage.

The man he was meeting was already a naturalist, outdoorsman, and writer in his own right, long before an accident of history—the assassination of President William McKinley—had thrust him into office as the youngest president in United States history. Roosevelt had learned taxidermy and become an expert on birds as a child in New York City, and he had developed a love of hunting big game—bison, elk, bear, bighorn sheep, Rocky Mountain goats—during several years as a rancher in the Dakotas, where he had found solace in the open spaces of the West while grieving the deaths of his wife and mother. Roosevelt had founded the Boone and Crockett Club with George Bird Grinnell, and transformed it from a rich man's sporting club to a force for conservation that helped create the National Zoo in Washington, D.C., set aside the Adirondack Forest Preserve in upstate New York, and passed legislation that put an end to poaching in Yellowstone.

As Governor of New York, Roosevelt had fought his own millinery industry to stop the slaughter of plumed birds in the Everglades; and after assuming the presidency, he had unilaterally created the nation's first wildlife refuge, Pelican Island, one of fifty-one he would declare while in office. He had also signed the laws establishing Crater Lake and Wind Cave National Parks (two of the five he would ultimately help create, doubling the number of national parks during his presidency). In the midst of his whirlwind cross-country tour, Roosevelt had spent a few weeks with John Burroughs in

Theodore Roosevelt had developed a love for Nature and the "vigorous life" as a young man in the West.

Yellowstone National Park, a place he had visited as a younger man, and he made a brief stop at the Grand Canyon, a sight he had never seen before but recognized immediately as a place needing greater federal protection. "Leave it as it is," he advised the people of Arizona. "The ages have been at work on it, and man can only mar it."

Roosevelt was, in other words, a kindred spirit. The fact that he was now president meant that the prospect of spending some days and nights alone with him in Yosemite was the opportunity of a lifetime for a proselytizer like Muir. Muir could preach his gospel of Nature—saving the forests, preserving the most special places as national parks, and turning Yosemite Valley and the Mariposa Grove back to the federal government—to a congregation of one: the most powerful man in the country. Compared with this opportunity, the missed chance of camping for a night with Ralph Waldo Emerson under the big trees thirty years earlier meant nothing.

But the start of the trip had to be disappointing. At the railroad station in Raymond on May 15, Muir was placed in an eleven-passenger open stage wagon with the president—along with the Governor of California, the Secretary of the Navy, the Surgeon General, two college presidents, and Roosevelt's personal secretary. Another similar-sized wagon carried

Muir could preach his gospel of Nature . . . to a congregation of one: the most powerful man in the country.

more staff and dignitaries. A detachment of thirty African American troopers from the Ninth Cavalry rode along as escorts.

They stopped the lead wagon for a photograph at the Wawona Tunnel Tree; in it, Roosevelt is discernible only because he's standing up in the front seat, so his head peeps over the rest of the crowd. Later the entourage got out at the other "must stop" for all tourists, the base of the Grizzly Giant, for another official photograph; in this one, each person is easily distinguishable, with Muir looking a little drawn and forlorn, as if by now he was wondering whether this was the president's idea of being "out in the open with you."

Then Roosevelt sent the troops, the reporters and photographers, and virtually all of the official party back to the Wawona Hotel, where a series of receptions and a banquet were scheduled in the president's honor that evening. They left expecting that Roosevelt would soon be joining them. In that, they were sorely mistaken. He had no intention of suffering through an endless round of political chitchat, a dinner with speeches, and another night in a hotel bed. He and Muir were now exactly where he had wanted to be: essentially alone in a forest of giant sequoias—except for an army packer named Jackie Alder and two park rangers, Archie Leonard and Charles Leidig (the son of one of the early hotel owners in the Valley and

President Theodore Roosevelt (standing in his carriage, peeking over the others) and his entourage of dignitaries pause at the Wawona Tunnel Tree in the Mariposa Grove.

the first white male born there), who went to work setting up a camp. After a short nap and a supper of fried chicken and beefsteak with a few cups of strong coffee that Leidig prepared, Roosevelt sat down by a blazing fire as twilight enveloped the grove. He and Muir began talking. With the Grizzly Giant silently presiding, the most important camping trip in American history was under way.

Each man later noted some differences between them. "Muir cared little for birds or bird songs," Roosevelt the ornithologist-president wrote. Muir, in turn,

Above: Still surrounded by his official party, Roosevelt (center, with Muir to his left) poses at the base of the Grizzly Giant.

Opposite: After their second night of camping together, Roosevelt and Muir stand at Glacier Point.

could not help tweaking the president, twenty years his junior, for his reputation as a big-game hunter. "Mr. Roosevelt," he asked, "when are you going to get beyond the boyishness of killing things?" But the two men had much more in common, and the glow of the campfire and the embers floating toward the lofty canopy of ancient trees seems to have cast a spell on them. "The night was clear," Roosevelt remembered, and "in the darkening aisles of the great sequoia grove . . . the majestic trunks, beautiful in color and symmetry, rose round us like the pillars of a mightier cathedral than ever was conceived even by the fervor of the Middle Ages. Hermit thrushes sang beautifully in the evening." Muir wrote his wife: "I had a perfectly glorious time. I never before had a more interesting, hearty, and manly companion. I stuffed him pretty well regarding the timber thieves, the destructive work of the lumbermen, and other spoilers of the forest." To a friend, Muir added: "Camping with the President was a remarkable experience. I fairly fell in love with him."

After spending the night on a bed made of a pile of army blankets, placed under a shelter-half, Roosevelt wanted an early start the next morning. He was particularly eager, Leidig said, to avoid the Wawona Hotel "for fear the President would be brought in contact with the members of his own official party." They saddled up, and Leidig led them down the Lightning Trail toward Yosemite Valley. Nearing Sentinel Dome, they all took turns breaking trail through the remaining winter snow. At one point it was five feet deep, and when the president got mired in the drifts, Leidig had to help him out with a log. A late spring storm whipped up—a hard snow driven by the wind—and they were tired but grateful when they stopped and made camp at a spot Leidig suggested not far from Glacier Point.

This was a much different setting, high above the Valley, cold and snowy, than the tranquil night before. But these were two experienced outdoorsmen more often exhilarated than discouraged by rough weather. The campfire that night drew them deeper in conversation. "Roosevelt and Muir talked far into the night regarding Muir's glacial theory of the formation of Yosemite Valley," Leidig recalled. "They talked a great deal about the conservation of forests in general and Yosemite in particular." Equally significant, Leidig "heard them discussing the setting aside of other areas in the United States for park purposes."

What a conversation it must have been—and just what Muir had hoped for. Leidig's report makes clear that restoring Yosemite Valley and the Mariposa Grove to the federal government was high on Muir's list, but only part of his agenda. What the "other

Roosevelt, Muir, and their camp tenders ride through the Valley
for their last campsite near Bridalveil Fall.

areas in the United States" were that they discussed in terms of future parks isn't recorded, but it's hard to imagine that the Grand Canyon wasn't one of them. Roosevelt had just made his first visit there; Muir had just waxed eloquently about it in print, calling it "a gigantic statement for even Nature to make." (They surely discussed Mount Shasta, because within days of the trip, as soon as he had access to a telegraph, the president wired his Secretary of the Interior, telling him to extend the federal forest reserve north from Yosemite to embrace Shasta.) Whatever was on the list, the discussion was so intense, Leidig said, that "some difficulty was encountered because both men wanted to do the talking."

They awoke the next morning under a fresh coating of five inches of snow. Rather than feeling inconvenienced, Roosevelt was thrilled. "We slept in a snowstorm last night!" he exclaimed to people he met later on May 17. "This has been the grandest day of my life." On Glacier Point, with the Valley and Yosemite Falls arrayed at their feet, the two men posed for an official photograph. Both appear resolute. "They have just agreed," the historian Donald Worster wrote, "that ownership of the much-abused valley below should revert to the federal government and become part of Yosemite National Park. Politically, they have forged a formidable alliance on behalf of nature." (Roosevelt would go on to become the greatest conservation president in American history, adding five new national parks, fifty-one bird sanctuaries, four national game refuges, eighteen national monuments, and, often in the face of fierce congres-

sional opposition, one hundred million combined acres of national forest. Under his leadership, more than two hundred eighty thousand square miles of federal land—an area larger than the state of Texas—would be placed under one kind of conservation protection or another.)

From Glacier Point the small party rode to the Valley on the fourteen-mile trail via Nevada Fall. Large crowds greeted them at Camp Curry and along the Merced, where a huge "Welcome" banner hung over the iron bridge. The Yosemite commissioners and members of the official party, already jealous of the way Muir had seemingly monopolized the president's time, eagerly awaited their own turns at having Roosevelt's ear. A chef, brought in from the Bohemian Club in San Francisco, was preparing a gourmet feast to be followed by four hundred dollars' worth of fireworks and then a grand illumination of Yosemite Falls by special calcium searchlights. An artist's studio had been converted into Roosevelt's private overnight lodging, with a warm bed and a cozy feather mattress.

This was the first time a sitting president had visited Yosemite Valley, and the state commissioners intended to make the most of it. Showing Roosevelt his sleeping quarters, they offered a champagne toast, and John Stevens, the Guardian of the Grant at the time, presented Roosevelt with the "key" to the Valley (carved from manzanita wood). Then, as the governor began outlining the elaborate plans for the night's festivities, the president interrupted: "We will pitch camp at Bridalveil!" His final night,

Roosevelt announced, would be spent camping one more time with John Muir, at the place Muir had recommended.

With that, the five members of the camping party mounted their horses again and rode off—followed by buggies and surreys and people filling the road on foot. (The group paused only a few times when Roosevelt, impatient to be away from the crowds, nonetheless stopped to say hello to an old friend from the Rough Riders' adventures in Cuba, or to pick up a little girl holding a flag and tell her, "God bless you, you little angel," or to scold another youngster who had the audacity to call him "Teddy.") Once they reached the campsite—at the edge of Bridalveil Meadow just west of the waterfall, with El Capitan and Ribbon Fall on the other side of the Merced—Leidig was asked to disperse the throng, estimated at between five hundred and a thousand people, all swarming in to catch a peek at the president. He told them Roosevelt was tired and wanted to be alone, and "they went," he said, "some of them even on tiptoe, so as not to annoy the president."

While Leidig cooked the final supper ("Charlie, I am as hungry as Hell," Leidig remembered Roosevelt saying. "Cook any damn thing you wish."), Roosevelt napped on his blankets for half an hour, snoring so loudly Leidig could hear him above the

And Roosevelt had now been exposed to the wilderness prophet of the Range of Light. . . . No one was immune from that.

crackling fire. After the meal Roosevelt and Muir strolled the meadow, through sunset and into the night. By the time they returned, they had apparently thoroughly exhausted their conservation conversations, because the topic around the final campfire was Roosevelt's tales of lion hunting, not exactly something Muir was interested in. Early the next morning, the twice-jilted official party picked up the president, and the stage rushed him back to his special train in Raymond, covering the sixty-seven miles in ten hours of actual driving time—a record never equaled in the era of horse-drawn vehicles.

Roosevelt returned to his whirlwind tour; Muir returned to his writing desk. But the camping trip's significance would reverberate into the future. Muir now had a friend in the Oval Office, someone he could go to on issues concerning not just Yosemite but all of America's remaining natural treasures. And Roosevelt had now been exposed to the wilderness prophet of the Range of Light, the John the Baptist of the River of Mercy. No one was immune from that.

"John Muir talked even better than he wrote," Roosevelt observed years later. "His greatest influence was always upon those who were brought into personal contact with him." That influence would be compromised in the future, over the fate of Hetch Hetchy, but it was still shining brightly a few days after the trip, when the president made his views clear about the recession of the Yosemite Grant in the state capital of Sacramento:

> Lying out at night under those Sequoias was lying in a temple built by no hand of man, a temple grander than any human architect could by any possibility build, and I hope for the preservation of the groves of giant trees simply because it would be a shame to our civilization to let them disappear. They are monuments in themselves. . . . I want them preserved.
>
> In California I am impressed by how great the State is, but I am even more impressed by the immensely greater greatness that lies in the future, and I ask that your marvelous natural resources be handed on unimpaired to your posterity. We are not building this country of ours for a day. It is to last through the ages.

With a president as vigorous as Theodore Roosevelt on the side of recession, it might seem like an easy thing to accomplish. Such was not the case, however. The president wanted the Yosemite Grant back, but would the state give it up? That was now the issue. The state commission had been so thoroughly discredited that many California leaders, including the governor, supported turning the Valley and giant sequoias back to the federal government. But opposition to the idea was still strong in some places, including the state legislature.

The San Francisco Examiner took up a crusade to stop what it called the "scheme to take Yosemite away from California." It persuaded the state's Board of Agriculture to formally oppose recession, and it began running regular stories that prominently

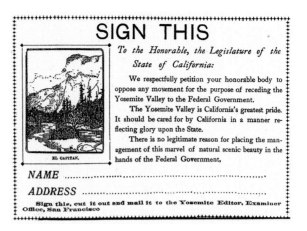

The San Francisco Examiner printed these petitions for readers to sign, opposing the return of Yosemite Valley to the federal government. Some 62,890 people responded.

quoted other opponents. *The Examiner* also printed petitions for its readers to cut out and sign and send back, for the newspaper to present to the legislature. "The Yosemite Valley," the petition said, "is California's greatest pride. It should be cared for by California in a manner reflecting glory on the state."

But many other state newspapers endorsed recession, most often on the grounds that the state had clearly demonstrated that it couldn't provide the Yosemite Grant with the financial support it needed, and that the federal model in the high country, with the army in charge, simply worked better. Putting everything into a single national park, they argued, would save the state money and ensure better protection for Yosemite's treasures, and California could have all the economic benefits of a world-class tourist attraction without paying for any of it from the state treasury.

The battle reached its peak in Sacramento in early 1905. When the assembly passed a recession bill, *The Examiner* announced it had collected 62,890 signed petitions against it, and after counting heads in the state's upper chamber confidently proclaimed: "Recession Is Beaten in the Senate." The rival *San Francisco Chronicle* responded with an interview with John Muir, his photograph, and highlighted quotations from him in favor of the bill. But what may have turned the tide was something other than Muir's eloquence or the dozen trips he made to Sacramento to lobby for recession. It was another powerful individual Muir had met in person: Edward Harriman, host of the Alaska cruise of 1899, who had recently added the Southern Pacific Railroad to his empire. After receiving a letter from Muir about the situation in Sacramento, Harriman instructed his minions in California, where the railroad was rumored to "own" a good share of the senate, to help out behind the scenes.

Whatever ultimately motivated them, on February 23, 1905, twenty-one senators voted in favor of the recession bill; thirteen voted against it. Nine of the senators voting for passage had previously been identified as opponents. On March 3, Governor George Pardee, who had been part of the official party that accompanied President Roosevelt to Yosemite in 1903, signed the bill into law. Because of some procedural delays and complicated maneuverings about another boundary adjustment (this time, the Southern Pacific's interests did not coincide with Muir's), Congress did not formally accept the recession for another year and a half. President Roosevelt signed it on June 11, 1906.

The seed of the park idea that had been planted in Yosemite forty-two years earlier not only had grown enough to spread to other locales, it had now repropagated itself, in its new form, in its original locale. There was no longer a park within a park. There was just Yosemite *National* Park—and it was part of a budding system of national parks. Muir had been fighting for this since 1890. Even after President Roosevelt's promise of support on Glacier Point, it had taken another three long years. "Sound the timbrel," Muir wrote a friend, "and let every Yosemite tree and stream rejoice!"

> I am now an experienced lobbyist; my political education is complete. Have attended [the] Legislature, made speeches, explained, exhorted, persuaded every mother's son of the legislators, newspaper reporters, and everybody else who would listen to me.
>
> And now that the fight is finished and my education as a politician and lobbyist is finished, I am almost finished myself.

◄◦►

BUT THE FIGHT WASN'T FINISHED. Part of Yosemite's story in the evolution of the national park idea—and perhaps one of the most important lessons embedded in it—is that the fight is *never* finished. A sacred place can be ruined forever, but it can never really be preserved forever. It can only be saved as long as the next threat is defeated—and the threat after that, and the one after that, and so on, down

Muir considered the beautiful Hetch Hetchy Valley a "precious
mountain temple." San Francisco wanted to build a dam and
entomb it all under a huge water reservoir.

through the generations. As Muir would soon learn, and express in his own way: "The battle for conservation will go on endlessly. It is part of the universal warfare between right and wrong." And "right" does not automatically win the battle.

In 1906, the same year all of Yosemite became a national park, a tremendous earthquake struck San Francisco, leveling hundreds of buildings and igniting fires that consumed most of the city, killing thousands of people. Out of the devastation came a renewed push to put a dam on the Tuolumne River in Hetch Hetchy Valley to create a better supply of water to San Francisco. Such a plan was a sacrilege in Muir's eyes: the city had other alternatives than entombing under hundreds of feet of water a place he considered equal to Yosemite Valley, perhaps even better because it was still undeveloped. Muir had specifically included it in his proposed boundaries for the high-country national park, thinking by doing so, it would be safe from despoliation. For years, with the help of Roosevelt's administration, he had successfully fended off three attempts by the city to get federal permission for a dam and reservoir within a national park.

In the wake of the earthquake, the momentum shifted in San Francisco's favor. Political leaders claimed that Hetch Hetchy's water could have spared the city from the devastating fires. It wasn't true, but with San Francisco reduced to ashes, arguing otherwise was highly unpopular. Muir made the fight anyway. "Dam Hetch Hetchy!" he thundered. "As well dam for water-tanks the people's cathedrals and

churches, for no holier temple has ever been consecrated by the heart of man." San Francisco's mayor responded by maligning Muir and his motives. "John Muir loves the Sierras and roams at large, and is hypersensitive on the subject of the invasion of *his* territory," the mayor said. "The four hundred thousand people of San Francisco are suffering from bad water and ask Mr. Muir to cease his aesthetic quibbling." Cartoons portrayed him as a fussy old woman in a dress, sweeping furiously with a broom against the tide of the project.

City residents voted seven to one in favor of the dam; even Muir's own Sierra Club split over the issue, with some prominent members advocating for it. In Washington, D.C., Gifford Pinchot, the nation's top forester and President Roosevelt's trusted adviser, threw his support behind the project. The president himself, despite a personal appeal from his old Yosemite camping buddy, refused to intervene. "I will do everything in my power to protect not only Yosemite, which we have already protected, but other similar great natural beauties of this country," Roosevelt wrote Muir, "but you must remember that it is out of the question permanently to protect them unless we have a certain degree of friendliness toward them on the part of the people of the State in which they are situated."

Roosevelt's waffling was a huge disappointment, but Muir did not give up. In 1909, when the new president, William Howard Taft, came to California, he asked that Muir be his guide for his own tour of Yosemite. Muir's personal touch was persuasive once more: after the visit Taft decided to oppose the Hetch Hetchy dam. By 1913, however, yet another president, Woodrow Wilson, had taken office; his new Secretary of the Interior was San Francisco's former city attorney, and the dam proposal was back on track.

Muir had come to believe that Hetch Hetchy's vulnerability was at least partly due to the small number of people who had actually seen it. Yes, it was far more pristine than the much-visited Yosemite Valley, but it had fewer passionate friends. President Taft's Secretary of the Interior—the first high-level federal official to actually see Hetch Hetchy—had come away firmly opposed to turning it into a water reservoir. Harriet Monroe, a prominent Chicago editor whom Muir had recruited into the leadership of the newly formed Society for the Protection of National Parks, became a powerful spokesperson for the cause after visiting Hetch Hetchy herself. But it needed more allies, and in Muir's mind that meant more people needed to experience his "precious mountain temple," not just hear or read about it.

Muir proposed building an expanded road network for the park, a "grand circular drive" that would link Yosemite Valley, Tuolumne Meadows in the high country, and Tuolumne Canyon down to Hetch Hetchy Valley, creating what he called "one of the grandest drives" in the world. Nor was Muir opposed to automobiles, which the army had banned from the park. They were "useful, progressive, blunt-nosed mechanical beetles," he said, who might "mingle their gas-breath with the breath of the pines and waterfalls," but with the proper restrictions on

John Muir: "The battle for conservation will go on endlessly."

their use, automobiles could convey more people to places where the encounter with Nature would perform their necessary conversion into park advocates. "Heaven knows," he wrote, "that John [the] Baptist was not more eager to get all his fellow sinners into the Jordan than I to baptize all of mine in the beauty of God's mountains."

It was all too late. On December 19, 1913, President Wilson signed the bill allowing work to begin on the dam that would ultimately bury Hetch Hetchy Valley under a vast reservoir. Muir was seventy-five, exhausted from the long battle, and brokenhearted by his loss. "It is hard to bear," he wrote some friends. "But in spite of Satan & Co. some sort of compensation must surely come out of even this dark damn-dam-damnation." A year later, Muir came down with pneumonia, and on Christmas Eve he died.

◂○▸

WITH THE PASSING OF JOHN MUIR, the growing national conservation movement had lost its clearest and most well-respected voice. Yosemite had lost its adopted son and ardent defender. But new defenders would rise up to replace him. As Muir predicted, "some sort of compensation" came from the loss of Hetch Hetchy. Another seed planted in Yosemite would grow and evolve into an important part of the national park idea. For years, advocates had been complaining that three different federal departments—Agriculture, Interior, and the Army—had some share of the responsibility for the national parks, which in truth meant no one was in charge. Nothing proved it more, they said, than Hetch Hetchy. They wanted a single agency entrusted with protecting the parks and making sure something like that never happened again. It was a broad-based effort, but the outrage over Hetch Hetchy galvanized it, and a new leader with connections to both Muir and Yosemite turned it into a crusade.

Stephen Mather was a promotional genius and self-made millionaire who had discovered what Frederick Law Olmsted had declared so emphatically in his Yosemite report of 1865: time spent in Nature was the best cure for frayed nerves and emotional exhaustion. In 1912, in what he always considered a highlight of his life, Mather had met John Muir on a Sierra Club hike and listened for hours as the old man rhapsodized about the healing powers of Nature and angrily denounced the plans for a dam at Hetch Hetchy.

In 1914, during a visit to Yosemite and Sequoia National Parks, Mather became disgusted at the conditions he saw: hiking trails in poor condition, cattle grazing where park rules supposedly prohibited it, and speculators misusing federal laws to file claims on choice parcels of big trees, which Mather believed should be protected forever. He dashed off a letter complaining to the new Secretary of Interior under President Wilson who was already under siege from conservationists because of his ruling on Hetch Hetchy. "If you don't like the way the national parks are being run," the secretary responded, "why don't you come down to Washington and run them yourself." Mather took him up on the offer—and the arc of park history changed in that moment.

Using his connections with influential people, his creative brilliance, and his prodigious energy, Mather mounted a campaign that soon had newspapers and magazines clamoring for creation of a new park agency. School children were writing essays about the national parks. Members of the General Federa-

Muir's disciple Stephen Mather turned the outrage over Hetch Hetchy into a crusade for a National Park Service, and became its first director.

This Nation is richer in natural scenery of the first order than any other nation, but it does not know it.

It possesses an empire of grandeur and beauty which it scarcely has heard of. It owns the most inspiring playgrounds and the best equipped nature schools in the world and is serenely ignorant of the fact.

In its national parks it has neglected, because it has quite overlooked, an economic asset of incalculable value.

The Nation must awake, and it now becomes our happy duty to waken it to so pleasing and profitable a reality.

Mather's economic argument for national parks won the day, and on August 25, 1916, the National Park Service was born, with Mather as its first director. Before his career ended in 1928, he would go on to create a legacy within the national parks arguably equal to that of his hero John Muir—so substantial that in every national park there is a plaque with Mather's likeness and these words: "There will never come an end to the good that he has done."

Solidifying the Yosemite connection to the birth of Park Service was the author of the key passage in the legislation creating it: Frederick Law Olmsted Jr., groomed by his father in the practice and philosophy of landscape architecture. As the nuts and bolts of the Park Service bill were being drafted, the group doing the work turned to the younger Olmsted to add "the essential thing . . . the reason it is worthwhile"—a statement of purpose meant to stand the test of time and guide park policy into the unseen future. The "fundamental purpose"

tion of Women's Clubs were writing their elected representatives. And Mather was personally lobbying members of Congress with the argument that only under a single government agency could the parks be properly managed and promoted. From Muir and the loss of Hetch Hetchy, he had learned that "nothing dollarable" is safe. Mather's solution was to argue that scenic treasures were also economic treasures:

Claire Marie Hodges became the Park Service's first woman ranger.

of the new agency, Olmsted wrote, is to "conserve the scenery and the natural and historic objects and the wildlife" of the parks, and "provide for the enjoyment of the same in such manner . . . as will leave them unimpaired for the enjoyment of future generations." With those words, Olmsted was restating the principles his father had enunciated fifty-one years earlier in Yosemite Valley and enshrining them into law.

As Mather expanded the number of parks, the army's soldiers were replaced by park rangers, who Mather molded into a cadre of professionals in distinctive flat-brimmed hats, equally proficient in their outdoors skills and ability to deal with the public.

Most of the rangers were men, but in Yosemite, when World War I made finding male rangers difficult, Claire Marie Hodges, who had been riding the park's trails since age fourteen, became the Park Service's first woman ranger.

Yosemite also led the way in many other respects for the evolving national park system. Under the prodding of Professor Joseph Grinnell at the University of California–Berkeley, the park was the first to establish an official program of field interpretation—guided nature walks and evening campfire lectures by "ranger naturalists"—that quickly spread to other parks and became one of the Park Service's most popular programs. The Yosemite Museum, completed in 1925, was the first of its kind in the park system—and the partnership that created it, the first nonprofit cooperating association for the Park Service, would serve as a national model.

In the 1930s a young Yosemite naturalist, George Melendez Wright, proposed a scientific survey of wildlife conditions in the park system and offered to finance it himself. His effort, which found that park managers were paying more attention to visitor amenities than to the equilibrium of nature, led to the creation of a new wildlife division (with Wright as its head), and ultimately a dramatic shift in Park Service policies. Predators would no longer be systematically eliminated; bears and other wild animals would no longer be treated as pets. Nature itself would be considered as important as the scenery—and left alone.

Photography and art, which had played such a critical role in both bringing Yosemite to the nation's attention and persuading Congress to preserve the Valley and giant sequoias, would continue as a vital part of the park's bloodstream. Painters like Chiura Obata would bring the beauty of Yosemite to the public's attention (and find its vivid memory important to surviving his darkest hours in a Japanese American internment camp during World War II). Photographers like Ansel Adams would not

Above: Chiura Obata found inspiration for his art and his life in Yosemite.

Left: Naturalist George Melendez Wright redirected Park Service policies to give Nature greater consideration.

only inspire people with their stunning pictures, but also use those photographs to rally the public for the park's protection.

Other patterns that had been visible from Yosemite's start also continued through time. While federal jurisdiction significantly improved the park's management, it would never receive adequate funding for its maintenance and improvement. Someone else would have to fill the gap. Just as Frederick Law Olmsted paid for the first survey of the Yosemite Grant with his own money, and Galen Clark continued working as Guardian of the Grant when he wasn't paid, dedicated citizens would continue to step forward with their time and money whenever Yosemite needed it most. Stephen Mather and some friends purchased the Tioga Road from its private owners and gave it to the nation as part of the park. Yosemite would always be Mather's favorite park, and in 1920 he dipped again into his own pocket for construction of the Ranger's Club in the Valley, providing park rangers with better accommodations. (It would be completed in 1924 and is now a National Historic Landmark.)

A nation's most magnificent and sacred places should be preserved for everyone and for all time.

This spirit of philanthropy and civic involvement continued long after Mather's passing. In 1961 Mary Curry Tresidder, daughter of the founders of Camp Curry, and her husband, Don, donated the money for Sunrise High Sierra Camp, completing the facilities for the fifty-mile High Sierra Camp loop on the belief that people should have better access to the mountains that had inspired John Muir. Citizen groups, like Yosemite Conservancy, would band together to help the National Park Service build new trails, preserve critical habitat, conduct educational programs, and in the twenty-first century embark on an ambitious restoration project to bring the Mariposa Grove closer to what Galen Clark had first encountered in 1857.

And the seed first planted in 1864 with the Yosemite Grant would grow, like a mighty sequoia, and branch out into a system of national parks encompassing more than four hundred individual sites, covering eighty-four million acres in the United States—and even more, as countries across the world copied the American notion that a nation's most magnificent and sacred places should be preserved for everyone and for all time. In his book *The Yosemite*, John Muir had predicted that, too:

> Everybody needs beauty as well as bread, places to play in and pray in, where Nature may heal and cheer and give strength to body and soul alike. This natural beauty-hunger is made manifest in . . . our magnificent National Parks—Nature's sublime wonderlands, the admiration and joy of the world.

Ansel Adams used his photographs (like *Moon and Half Dome*, opposite) to rally people on Yosemite's behalf.

INSPIRATION
POINT

DRIVING TO YOSEMITE VALLEY after my visit with the Grizzly Giant in the Mariposa Grove, I made a sweeping turn to the right, kept descending on the highway, and approached a black hole in the side of a mountain. The Wawona Tunnel swallowed my car. I turned on the headlights and penetrated the tube of darkness, which extends more than four-fifths of a mile through solid granite. There was, as the saying goes, a light at the end of the tunnel, but when I reached it the light was much more than a return to daylight. It was a revelation. The tunnel exit was a huge arched frame, dramatically presenting the first view of the Valley.

Ah-wah-nee, the place of the gaping mouth, opened before my eyes. The frothy white ribbon of Bridalveil Fall, seemingly almost within touch on the right, plunged over a cliff edge in front of the three angled incisors of Cathedral Rocks. The hulking molar of El Capitan crowded in on the left, yet leaving enough of a gap to peer deeper down the Valley's throat, beyond the two opposing jaws to the long tongue of Clouds Rest, with Half Dome peeking up at its tip. I pulled onto the broad balcony of a parking lot and got out for a longer look.

This was essentially the same view that had stopped Lafayette Bunnell in his tracks with the Mariposa Battalion in 1851, where he saw and felt the "testimony of the rocks" that first set things in motion for the eventual birth of the national park idea. Bunnell's recital of the testimony had attracted James Mason Hutchings to the same vantage point,

George Fiske's photograph from Inspiration Point in the 1880s

which Hutchings compared to both biblical scripture and Niagara Falls, which in turn brought photographers and artists to the scene, and Galen Clark, who added the sequoia grove to the tableau. The photographs, the paintings, those enormous trees, and the promptings of people whose names are lost to history had somehow created the conditions for something new under the sun: the notion that views as spectacular as these should belong to everyone for all time. This is where the seed of the future was first planted 150 years ago, with no one knowing for sure whether it would grow to maturity, or what it would become if it did.

The view of the Valley—of granite monoliths, a carpet of evergreens, and a sacramental pouring

of water—evokes a sense of both permanence and freshness, simultaneously breathtaking and tranquil, unchanging and dynamic, what the writer Fitz Hugh Ludlow described in 1870 as "a new heaven and a new earth into which the creative spirit had just been breathed." It seems only natural and right that such a place would be preserved; it seems self-evident it would become a national park. But my time with the Grizzly Giant and its brethren had taught me that between the seed and the big tree, nothing is self-evident and certain. The way things are is just one version of the way things could have turned out.

What if history had proceeded differently? What if James Mason Hutchings had not read about a waterfall bigger than Niagara's; had instead been content to publicize the Calaveras Big Trees, with the stump that doubled as a ballroom floor and the

stripped-down "Mother of the Forest"; had decided to begin rather than end his career as a hotelier there? What if, for whatever reason, no one had asked Congress in 1864 to create the Yosemite Grant and entrust it to the state of California? What if Frederick Law Olmsted had simply presided over a failed mining venture in the Sierra foothills before returning to New York City's Central Park at the end of the Civil War? What if John Muir had gone to Brazil as planned instead of California in 1868; or what if he had encountered a Yosemite Valley already carved into a multitude of private homesteads with perhaps a small town at its center? What if the wonders of Yellowstone had been laid before the nation's lawmakers in 1872 without any precedent whatsoever for treating such a place as anything but yet another parcel of land best turned into private property, just like every other part of the public domain? Without the Yosemite Grant, would America have ever come up with the revolutionary idea of national parks and developed them into something Muir proudly called "the admiration and joy of the world"?

It's impossible to say. Maybe people and events would have brought us to the same place. Then again, maybe not. It's not at all difficult to imagine a number of alternative histories, none of which provides the combination of conditions resulting in what

It's not at all difficult to imagine a number of alternative histories. . . .

became America's best idea. It's even easier to know what America would be like without the national parks that grew from that idea.

The rim of the Grand Canyon would be lined with McMansions, each one with a multimillion-dollar view—and each one with a No Trespassing sign in front. Regular citizens would never have the chance to stand at the canyon's edge in hushed awe as they contemplate an immensity of time and space that staggers the imagination. At the canyon's bottom would not be a free-running river but a reservoir providing water and electricity to Las Vegas. The Everglades, where a dizzying diversity of plant and animal life now thrives, would have been drained long ago, then paved and turned into shopping centers and condominium complexes. Yellowstone would be a gaudy amusement park called Geyser World. Some of its thermal features would have been tapped for their energy. Deprived of their last refuge at a time when their once uncountable numbers had been reduced to several dozen, the bison would have gone the way of the passenger pigeon and become extinct. There would be no wolves within the Lower 48 states.

And Yosemite? Without the protection that came with the Yosemite Grant and ultimate national park, the ancient sequoias of the Mariposa Grove would have suffered the fate of the nearby Nelder Grove, also "discovered" by Galen Clark: 80 percent of the mature trees turned into fence posts and

Opposite: Thomas Hill's *The Yosemite Valley*, 1888.

pencils during the great logging boom of the late 1800s. Perhaps the Grizzly Giant would have been spared, because of the dark cavity at its base and its less-than-straight trunk, making it a lonely sentinel of a lost race awkwardly waving its massive arms at no one in particular; or perhaps it would have been the first to be felled, because it's already leaning toward the ground. Yosemite's high country would have remained open to over-grazing and logging; without the trees and grasses to trap and hold the winter snows, the springtime melts would be swifter and the clear streams would be clogged with silt.

The Valley itself, which so many people have considered a cathedral designed by Nature, could just as easily have been considered perfectly designed for a gated community. Imagine the championship golf courses in the meadows along the Merced, with a jaw-dropping backdrop to each hole. Imagine the asking price of a trophy home with a view out the picture window of morning light on Yosemite Falls or evening's alpenglow on Half Dome. Imagine just how many trophy homes with such views could be built in the Valley. Do the calculations and ask your-self if it would have remained Nature's cathedral. No, the Valley would have become a developer's paradise.

As far back as 1865, Frederick Law Olmsted, understanding human nature and the history that flows from it, had postulated such an alternative universe as an entirely possible future for Yosemite and

The seed of a new idea had finally sprouted.

special places like it. "Men who are rich enough," he reminded his fellow commissioners, "can and do pro-vide places of . . . needed recreation for themselves. They have done so from the earliest periods known in the history of the world." Citing the Babylonians, the Persians, the Hebrews, and the aristocracy of Europe, he noted that from the begin-nings of time, "the enjoyment of the choicest natural scenes in the country [becomes] a monopoly, in a very peculiar manner, of a very few, very rich people." That was the way the world had always worked.

Yet somehow, in Yosemite, a first tentative step was taken in a different direction, and the course of history was deflected toward a different, better future. Human nature didn't necessarily change, but the world no longer necessarily worked the way it always had. The seed of a new idea had finally sprouted. A century and a half ago, Olmsted was one of the few who understood how this new idea had evolved from the larger seedbed of democracy, how its lineage could be traced back to the nation's founding ideals of "life, liberty, and the pursuit of happiness." Olm-sted also understood how profound this new idea could be, if properly nurtured and allowed to grow. In 1865 he predicted that the hundreds then visiting Yosemite would soon become thousands, "and in a century the whole number of visitors will be counted by the millions." In 1965, on the centennial of his pronouncement, visitation hit 1.6 million. By 2012, as Yosemite approached its 150th birthday, the number of yearly visitors was nearing 4 million. That's the kind of growth that rivals a sequoia's.

◄○►

BUT SEQUOIAS ALSO REMIND US that most seeds do not germinate and sprout, and even those that do don't often grow to maturity. That, too, requires the right combination of circumstances. In the case of Yosemite and the national park idea, it required the right combination of people. It needed people like Hutchings and Clark, Olmsted and Muir and Roosevelt, and many others—promoters and caretakers, planners and prophets and politicians, and everyday citizens who simply loved the place enough to devote some portion of their energy to protecting it. For the idea to survive and thrive, their spirit must replenish it. It requires a fresh renewal every generation.

The Tunnel View overlook proves the point. A steep footpath climbs the mountainside behind the parking lot to overlooks called Inspiration Point and Old Inspiration Point, where earlier trails once brought generations of visitors to the Valley before the Wawona Tunnel was completed in 1933 at a lower elevation more conducive to a paved highway. Supervising the road and tunnel's construction was none other than Frederick Law Olmsted Jr. Just as he had when he wrote the bill creating the National Park Service in 1916, the younger Olmsted once again revived the spirit of his father's manifesto of 1865, especially its challenge to make the park accessible to as many people as possible, yet always to con-

sider the "dignity of the scenery" as the first duty. Olmsted Jr. insisted that all of the granite rubble blasted out of the mountain to create the tunnel be put to a better use than simply dumping it down the slope. Instead, he suggested they use all that rock to create an expansive overlook, a modern-day version of Inspiration Point, geared toward visitors arriving by automobile instead of by donkey, and arriving in far greater numbers.

Both Olmsteds would have appreciated the scene on the afternoon I was there. The overlook teemed with activity. Cars and tour busses were pulling in or pulling out and a constantly changing crowd of about 250 people milled along the stone balustrade. Rather than writing detailed notes on what they saw and felt, like visitors past, everyone was taking pictures and talking excitedly in a Babel of tongues: Japanese, Chinese, French, German, Spanish, Italian, Dutch, Norwegian, Swedish, Indian, British English, Australian English, and several indistinguishable Middle-European languages. The elder Olmsted's prophecy that Yosemite would become a worldwide tourist attraction had proven true. (So was his prediction that the park would be an economic boon to California and the nation: in 2010 the nearly four million visitors spent $354.7 million in the immediate area.) Following his father's example, the younger Olmsted had helped make it all possible, first by contributing to the creation of a federal agency with the sole mission of protecting such treasures, and second by designing a way for more people to experience one of them.

Historically it's up in the higher, rougher terrain of the older viewpoints where the inspiration first occurred and kept reoccurring, where one early visitor after another became awed by the view and struggled to describe what they all called indescribable. "Here," the early geologist Clarence King wrote in 1872, "all who make California books, down to the last and most sentimental specimen who so much as meditates a letter to his or her local newspaper, dismounts and inflates." Yosemite has had four "Inspiration Points" in its history; nearly five when park managers briefly considered attaching that name to the Tunnel View parking area, then decided against adding to the confusion. But the vista from the new overlook, regardless of its name and regardless that it was designed by man, not Nature, is essentially the same as the older Inspiration Points. It is just as inspirational—and much easier to reach.

The scene I witnessed was not history repeating itself exactly, but certainly replicating itself through adaptive evolution. The crucial thing—the essential DNA—was that inspiration still occurred because the view had been preserved by the creation of a park, and then the park had been protected by succeeding generations. In this instance, the generational connection was literal, father to son, but the park idea is a quintessentially democratic legacy and does not have to follow bloodlines.

Ranger Dean Shenk may not be Galen Clark's lineal descendant or incarnation (though he sports a similar gray beard), yet his devotion to the trees in the Mariposa Grove seems just as sincere and deep-

Dean Shenk, protector of the Mariposa Grove

rooted. He was a junior-college student studying art and photography when he came upon Yosemite. Like Clark, he was hooked from the start—beginning as a park volunteer in the early 1970s, then rising to become a full-fledged ranger who has worked on bear studies, patrolled the Valley (and broke up a fight between a man with a hunting knife and a biker with a steel chain), and finally moved to the Wawona/Mariposa Grove district, where like his hero Clark, Shenk personally inventoried the trees under his care. "I just didn't want to leave Yosemite," he told me. "Yosemite is a disease," he added, but as Clark discovered, it is also its own cure.

With her training as an ecologist fueling her enthusiasm to restore the Mariposa Grove (by protecting the ancient trees while encouraging new growth), Monica Buhler reminded me a little of John Muir.

His passion for Nature was inspired as much by his scientific studies as by his Transcendentalist readings.

I tramped the high country with another park ranger, Dick Ewart, who in the course of nearly forty years has become as intimately familiar with the Range of Light as John Muir. Ewart, too, fell in love with Yosemite from the moment he saw it in 1975. After joining a guided hike, he told the ranger who led it, "I want your job." He volunteered in the Yosemite Association's bookstore, unloading trucks and stocking shelves (supporting himself by working on cars), and read all of the visitor center's books in preparation for applying for a Park Service job. Though stationed now at Glacier Point, much of Ewart's career has been spent in Yosemite's alpine region, based at Tuolumne

Dick Ewart, high-country ranger

Meadows, where he still conducts long hikes into the park's wilderness and trains rangers to lead weeklong treks from one high-country camp to another.

At age sixty, Ewart is as lean and spry as Muir was, with leg muscles that look like knotted wood. Out on the trail he brims with enthusiasm whenever he stops (which is often) to identify a particular flower or tree, describe the glacial geology of a particular valley, glory in the beauty of a cascading stream, point out the distinctive "T" blazes still visible on trails created by the cavalry a hundred years ago, or survey a panorama of mountain peaks, insistent on naming each one and telling the story behind each name. (Instead of Muir's Scottish brogue, however, Ewart retains the accent of his native Massachusetts: a nighttime ranger discussion of the constellations is a "ranger tahhk about stahhs in the pahhk.")

Monica Buhler, restoration ecologist

In his early, younger days, Ewart felt compelled to replicate a number of Muir's well-recorded adventures: edging out along the lip of Upper Yosemite Fall as well as sneaking into the declivity at its thundering base; summiting the park's tallest peaks; spending the night on top of Half Dome (on the centennial of George Anderson's first ascent). But as much as he may embody Muir's spirit, Ewart's personal heroes are drawn from later generations, who themselves were Muir's spiritual heirs. Ewart idolizes Stephen Mather, the driving force behind the creation of the National Park Service and its first director. Mather's name and many contributions to the

The late Carl Sharsmith, legendary Yosemite ranger

park idea crop up in most of Ewart's campfire talks, whether they're the main topic or not, because, he said, "*Everybody* does John Muir—it's just Johnmuir, Johnmuir, Johnmuir—so I wanted to talk about some of the others."

One of those others comes from the generation after Mather: the legendary ranger-naturalist Carl Sharsmith, a biology professor who worked summers in the park from 1931 until he died in 1994, at age ninety-one the Park Service's oldest ranger. He had grown up reading Muir's books, copying his favorite passages into a notebook and rereading them until he had them memorized; he even named his son John in honor of the Mountain Prophet. Sharsmith's nature walks were renowned for the way he shared information with humor and passion, and he is credited with perhaps the most-repeated anecdote among park rangers. Asked by a visitor what he would do if he had only one day (in some retellings, it's only one hour) to spend in Yosemite, Sharsmith replied: "Madam, I'd go sit on a rock by the Merced River and I'd cry."

Ewart spent fourteen summers at Tuolumne Meadows in the tent next to Sharsmith's, and the older man became his good friend and mentor, infusing Ewart with the same dedication to science and quick wit with an audience. When Sharsmith was eighty-five, Ewart accompanied him on a camping trip to an unnamed 12,002-foot peak in the wilderness north of Tioga Pass, carrying his aged friend's tent and sleeping bag (as well as his own) as Sharsmith inched his way up the rugged trail to a meadow near the summit where he had discovered some rare alpine flowers many years earlier. They spent three days and two nights. There were moments, Ewart said, when he thought Sharsmith was going to die up there, "and that would have been okay" with both of them. Now, Ewart and other people in the park are trying to get the United States Board of Geographic Names to officially give the mountain the name Sharsmith Peak. Yosemite already has mountains and lakes named for politicians, celebrities, military officers and their wives, even European geologists who never came to the Sierra; Ewart and his cohorts figure that a man who devoted more than sixty years of his life to personally inspiring tens of thousands of tourists with his love and knowledge of Yosemite deserves similar recognition.

Down in Yosemite Valley, the evidence was equally palpable that the "creative spirit" of those who first planted the national park idea still lives. I spent a hot afternoon hiking to Mirror Lake with Pete Devine, the resident naturalist for Yosemite Conservancy. He's been teaching people about the park for a quarter century, and his fervor for the place shines in his bright eyes and is probably best expressed by his answer to a question on his blog: "Favorite Music? The Merced River." The waters of Yosemite sing to Devine as they once did to John Muir.

Mirror Lake formed centuries ago, after a rock fall produced an impediment in Tenaya Creek and the water backed up, creating a mile-long lake that became one of Yosemite's principal early attractions, with its stunning reflections of Half Dome

Pete Devine, naturalist and guide

and Mount Watkins. Slowly, the sand and silt and gravel washing down the creek settled in the lake's bottom. The lake began to shrink. The same process, Devine explained, created the meadows of Yosemite Valley from what had been a shallow lake behind a glacier's moraine fourteen thousand years ago. As all the streams pouring into the Valley deposited their debris, the Valley's lake became a succession of bogs and marshes, and ultimately rich-soil meadows with oaks and pines on the increasingly drier edges. All of that had occurred long before humans first entered the Valley.

In the case of Mirror Lake, early park managers, focusing on the scenic value of the lake's reflections, attempted to stop this natural progression. They built a small dam to raise the water level and regularly dredged out the sand (using it on the park roads in winter) to lower the bottom. But then the national park idea evolved in the middle of the twentieth century under the influence of Professor Joseph Grinnell and George Melendez Wright and finally the zoologist and conservationist A. Starker Leopold—all of whom urged that science play a larger role in decision-making. National parks, they argued, should preserve more than pretty scenery, and the emphasis gradually shifted toward letting Nature take its course. The same new thinking that brought an end to bear feedings, that finally ended the century-old spectacle of the "firefall" at Glacier Point, and that restored fire to the sequoia groves so that the species could regenerate, brought a new view of Mirror Lake. Park managers decided to stop trying to prevent Mirror Lake from becoming what it wants to become: Mirror Meadow.

With the dredging halted, what was once a mile-long lake is now a quarter mile in length. The former Upper Lake is now a collection of grassy marshes, and willows grow where none were evident when Devine first arrived in Yosemite. Beyond that, a pine forest has grown up. "I think it's quite exciting," he told me, "to witness geologic time in our own lifespan." Muir, who Devine likes to quote as often as possible, would approve. "Glaciers," he wrote in *The Yosemite*, "work apart from men. . . . Outspread, spirit-like, they brood above the predestined landscapes, work on unwearied through immeasurable ages, until, in the fullness of time, the mountains and valleys are brought forth, channels furrowed for rivers, basins made for lakes and meadows, . . . soils spread for forests and fields; then they shrink and vanish like summer clouds."

In Yosemite Village, I watched park ranger Shelton Johnson illuminate the story of the Buffalo Soldiers for a rapt crowd by in essence becoming one of the soldiers in a living-history performance. Dressed in a cavalryman's uniform from 1904, and quieting the crowd by playing on an Indian flute he had carved himself, he led us like The Pied Piper across a meadow, stopping occasionally to impart history and science by telling stories in the persona of Sgt. Elizy Bowman, a composite character he created from his research. Johnson's own story is a testament to the transformational power of national parks. Having been raised in Detroit's inner city, his first exposure was to Yellowstone, where he arrived by bus for a summer job with a concessionaire and ended up staying to become a park ranger. When he transferred to Yosemite and came across a faded photograph of some African American soldiers who were the park's earliest protectors, "it changed my life," he said. "They looked like me."

Johnson made it his mission to let more people know that people of color have been part of park history for a long time, and through that story remind them that the parks belong to them as much as any other Americans. With eloquence, enthusiasm, and an infectious sense of humor, he has now deliv-

Shelton Johnson, Buffalo Soldier reenactor

ered that message to millions of people, through his appearance in a PBS documentary and his role in attracting Oprah Winfrey to let him be her guide to Yosemite, an adventure she turned into two episodes of her popular television show. (Johnson's efforts earned him the Freeman Tilden Award, the highest honor the National Park Service bestows on interpretive rangers.) "I can't forget that little black kid in Detroit," he told me, "and other kids, just like me. How do I get them here—let them know that we, too, have a place here? Every time I go to work and put the uniform on, I think about them."

I spent a morning at the Yosemite Museum, near the park's visitor center. A short distance away,

Yosemite Falls pulsed over its lofty lip, the streaming white lifeblood of the park—what only recently had been snow in the Range of Light—joining all the other arteries that gather in the Valley. I could hear faint trills of children's laughter as they played in the spray and pools near the base of the falls. It reminded me of the story of Totuya's return in 1929, when the last survivor of the expulsion of Tenaya's band, in the midst of heartbreaking memories, found some solace, at least, in the fact that the falls still spoke to her as they had in her childhood. "Cho'-lok!" she had said. "Cho'-lok no gone!"

Inside the park museum, among the artifacts of Totuya's time, was living proof that native people aren't gone, either. Julia Parker was patiently weaving a basket out of sedge roots while a small crowd watched quietly. Of Miwok and Pomo ancestry, she married a man of Miwok and Paiute descent and moved to his home in Yosemite in 1949, where she learned the ancient methods of basket weaving from the local elders, including her husband's grandmother. Dedicated to passing along her knowledge just as she received it, Mrs. Parker has been demonstrating the skill at the museum since 1960; some of her baskets are displayed in the Smithsonian Institution and in the Windsor Castle collection of Queen Elizabeth (who visited in 1983). Mrs. Parker's hair is now snow white, but time hasn't slowed her nimble fingers. She bent over her work with extreme concentration, licking a thin strand of the sedge she had harvested and shaved, poking it with an awl through the tiny, tight spiral that would form a basket's center, pulling the new strand tight, and starting over with the next one, repeating a task she has done for more than half a century, a task that stretches back centuries more. A large, platter-sized basket might take a year and half to complete. After a few minutes of silent work, she looked up and laughed. "The start is always the hardest," she said. "And the end."

Outside the museum another park interpreter, Phil Johnson, a Miwok and Paiute descendant of the Valley's early inhabitants, led a tour of the reconstructed Indian village. He pointed out California redbuds and bracken ferns used for coloring baskets, spice bushes used for arrow shafts, examples of the cedar-bark *u-ma-chas* the Ahwahneechees once built for houses, and a larger, part-underground structure used for religious ceremonies. With a soft voice and

Julia Parker and one of her baskets

expressive hands, he knelt down to show us some mortar holes in a piece of granite. This is where his ancestors once pounded acorns, he said, and similar sites can still be found throughout the Valley—so-called gossip rocks, where women shared the village news as they worked together to prepare the tribe's principal sustenance, "nice, hot, acorn mush." He said those words in a way that made us all hungry and had us listening for the echo of the women's happy voices.

I walked across the street to visit Yosemite's cemetery, a large plot surrounded by incense cedars and a split-rail fence, where nearly fifty people were buried in the late 1800s and early 1900s. The graves are a representative sampling of the park's early years. James Lamon, who built the first winter cabin in the Valley, is buried there, as is George Anderson, who made the celebrated climb of Half Dome and installed the cable for others to follow. There are markers for stage drivers, guides, and storekeepers who made their livings in Yosemite, as well as some tourists who just happened to die there. Two of the deceased were murdered; another was a waitress who drowned in a boating accident on the Merced. One grave is signified by a wooden marker engraved simply "A Boy." One says only "Frenchman." Eleven of the graves are for Indians of the Valley, including some of Totuya's kin.

And then, of course, in one corner rests the giant granite slab and extra stone cross for the final resting place of James Mason Hutchings. His second wife and two daughters each get some space on different faces of the granite slab, but by far the biggest engraving calls him "Father of Yo Semite/Builder of the First Trails, Roads, Bridges and Dwellings of This Valley." The stone cross is simpler, restricting its honorifics to "Pioneer" and "Patriot." Hutchings always required a lot of adjectives.

But my interest was drawn to a smaller piece of rock closer to the cemetery's center. It's where Galen Clark had received permission to dig his own grave, place his own granite marker, and transplant some sequoia seedlings from the Mariposa Grove, which he patiently watered for decades in his declining years. Clark, it turns out, had always miscalculated his longevity. He had settled at Wawona in 1857 thinking he had mere months left to live, only to go on to bring the sequoias of the Mariposa Grove to the world's attention, become their doting caretaker, be named the Yosemite Grant's Guardian (twice), and hobnob with the likes of John Muir, Frederick Law Olmsted, Ralph Waldo Emerson, Civil War generals, famous politicians, and uncounted photographers who invariably included him in their pictures of the Grizzly Giant. In the winter of 1909–10 Clark finished writing *The Yosemite Valley: Its History, Characteristic Features and Theories Regarding Its Origin*, the third book he published in his nineties, which included this advice to Yosemite visitors: "A week is the shortest time that should be allowed for a trip to Yosemite. . . . The grandeur of the Valley cannot be fully appreciated in a few days." If anyone could testify to the park's rejuvenative powers and the reasons to linger, it was Clark. He died on March 24, 1910, four days shy of his ninety-sixth birthday. Yosemite had not only lengthened his life, it had deepened and expanded it immeasurably.

At his gravesite, where a chunk of granite simply states "Galen Clark, 1814–1910," is further evidence that even in death, Clark continues to return the favor: the four sequoia trees he had carefully dug up as seedlings, carried from the Mariposa Grove, planted back in the soil, and nurtured in hopes they would survive and grow to stand guard over his grave just as he had stood guard over their parents. Perhaps one of those parents was the Grizzly Giant. The trees are now roughly 150 years old, about the same age as the national park idea that began in Yosemite. Because of the interruption in sequoia regeneration that resulted from fire suppression during the park's first century, they are among the few sequoias we can say with much certainty are living benchmarks of that idea's growth from seed to tree.

Yosemite Conservancy volunteers restoring a meadow in the Valley

The Valley has a few other such transplants of similar age, and over the years—just like America's best idea—sequoias have been replanted all around the world (though none of the expatriates reproduce naturally). Giant sequoias can now be found in Turkey and Japan, Russia and Egypt, Australia and South America, and virtually every nation of Europe. Great Britain's largest tree is now a sequoia 8.5 feet in diameter and 150 feet tall, growing at Leon Castle north of Inverness; Europe's monarch sequoia, 13 feet in diameter, grows among its brethren on the

well-manicured palace grounds at La Granja, Spain, northwest of Madrid.

But the sequoias shading Clark's marker are closest to the original source. They're about 5 feet in diameter now and maybe 120 feet tall. Their shallow roots radiate out toward the rest of the cemetery, and they extend inward toward one another, through Clark's gravesite. "Molecule by molecule he's being converted into the sequoias," naturalist Pete Devine told me when I mentioned them, "rising through the sap to the sky! Well done, Galen Clark." Well done, indeed.

At its best, the national park idea connects us to something larger than ourselves. To a gigantic living organism or the sweep of eons written in the sculpted granite of a beautiful valley. To the lesson John Muir learned that "when we try to pick out anything by itself, we find it hitched to everything else in the universe." To the notion that what we have inherited from Nature we have also inherited from those who protected it, and therefore that it is our sacred obligation to pass on that legacy to our children. The national park idea nourishes us. If we're wise, we nourish it in return.

At its best, the national park idea connects us to something larger than ourselves.

Standing near Galen Clark's graveside trees, I mentally compared them to the much older, spectacularly larger Grizzly Giant, and I was reminded to think like a sequoia. At a century and a half, sequoias are only youngsters. Not until they reach the age of six hundred or so does their rate of vertical growth slow in comparison to the growth of their lateral branches, and their tops begin to broaden into the distinctive rounded crown of full maturity. Then they can live and thrive (and thicken) for many more centuries. A 150-year-old sequoia that has made it past the many pitfalls of its early years and does not face the impending threat of a lumberman has the life expectancy of 2,850 more years, perhaps even longer. Like the park idea, I realized, these trees before me were unquestionably impressive. But they are still youthful, still developing. With loving care, just think of what they—and America's national park idea—can become in the distant future: *truly* monumental.

AFTERWORD

The important story told in *Seed of the Future* focuses on individuals spiritually tied to Yosemite and how their efforts have laid the groundwork for Yosemite National Park, as well as other national and international parks. It's our hope that Dayton Duncan's eloquent and powerful account will help inspire you to come join us in providing for the future of Yosemite.

This book honors the legacy of Jack Walston and the Walston family, who continue to make a difference, collectively and individually, enhancing the enjoyment, preservation, and protection of Yosemite National Park.

Seventy years ago, in August of 1943, eight-year-old Jack Walston first experienced the magic of Yosemite National Park. He arrived with his mother, Nella Walston, and his older brother, Carl, in a green Packard touring car that the Yosemite Park and Curry Company used to bring visitors from the Merced train station. His journey would spark a passion for the park that led to innumerable return visits, family memories, close connections, and a lifetime of service.

Today, Jack's devotion and contagious enthusiasm for Yosemite inspires family members spanning several generations, many of his closest friends, and countless others he has never met.

As the first board chair of the Yosemite Institute, Jack provided visionary leadership and business savvy to the notion that the next generation of park stewards would come through a new program. Inspired and directed by Don Rees with the blessing of the National Park Service, it would offer high school students a week filled with outdoor science, adventure, and hands-on learning within the grand classroom of Yosemite. What began as a dream has become NatureBridge—the residential field science program in Yosemite and five other national park units, instilling park stewardship in more than a million students over the past forty years.

Jack's commitment to the park also has included service as a valued trustee on the Yosemite Conservancy Council and Board, and as a member of the Western Regional Advisory Committee of the National Park Service. Following in his footsteps, his daughters and their husbands also have pursued paths of service to the park.

Eldest daughter, Jennifer, savored her summer dream job in Yosemite during her college years, and later became engaged to her husband, Gregory Johnson, there. The park has remained an integral part of their family life through their involvement in Yosemite Conservancy, where they serve on the Council and Board and have generously given of their time and resources. Also, the Mariposa Grove Restoration Project benefits greatly from their leadership as cochairs, and Yosemite frequently provides a spectacular backdrop for Jennifer and Greg's family Christmas cards featuring their son, Charles (Chad).

Daughter Jill spent her career in the park, became engaged at the top of Sentinel Dome, and married a third-generation ranger, Cameron (Cam) Sholly, in the Yosemite Chapel. Cam now serves as an Associate Director of the National Park Service in Washington, D.C. Their son, Cole, has enjoyed trick-or-treating in costume as a Junior Park Ranger or a backcountry bear together with his cousin Chad at family Halloween festivities in the park.

Jack's youngest daughter, Leslie (who has twice camped overnight on the top of Half Dome), and her husband, Tom Watson III, a retired naval aviation officer, frequent the park. They recently introduced their son, Tommy, to skiing at Badger Pass. It's worth noting that Jack's three daughters, and now all three grandsons, have learned to ski on the gentle slopes at Badger Pass—a Walston right of passage.

Jack Walston's legacy demonstrates that one person has the power to make a dramatic difference, and we thank the Walston family for their generous support of this book. Together we honor the 150th anniversary of Abraham Lincoln's signing of the Yosemite Grant Act that set aside the Yosemite Valley and the Mariposa Grove for all people, and germinated the idea for the national parks.

For six years, I had the honor to serve as the Superintendent of Yosemite National Park, and in that time I developed a deep love and an enduring commitment to Yosemite. After my retirement, I was delighted to serve as President of The Yosemite Fund, which has since merged with the Yosemite Association to form Yosemite Conservancy.

Through the support of donors, Yosemite Conservancy provides grants and support to Yosemite National Park to help preserve and protect Yosemite today and for future generations. The work funded by Yosemite Conservancy is visible throughout the park, from trail rehabilitation to wildlife protection and habitat restoration. The Conservancy is dedicated to enhancing the visitor experience and providing a deeper connection to the park through outdoor programs, volunteering, and wilderness services. Thanks to dedicated supporters, the Conservancy has provided more than $80 million in grants to Yosemite National Park.

Yosemite Conservancy provides a great way for individuals to become stewards of Yosemite by supporting essential work that would not happen without help from our donors and friends. Help us provide the margin of excellence for Yosemite.

It is time to visit Yosemite—go for a hike in the Mariposa Grove, feel the mist from Vernal Fall, gaze up at Half Dome. Join us on this journey, and become a steward of Yosemite for the future.

—MIKE TOLLEFSON, PRESIDENT
YOSEMITE CONSERVANCY

ACKNOWLEDGMENTS

THIS BOOK WAS the idea of Mike Tollefson, president and CEO of Yosemite Conservancy and former superintendent of the park. It was a great idea; whether I've lived up to its potential is for others to judge, but I thank him for the opportunity. Many members of Yosemite Conservancy staff provided help whenever it was needed. In particular, I thank Nicole Geiger for shepherding the book to completion, as well as the team of editors and designers she assembled, and Pete Devine, for guiding me on two unforgettable hikes to Mirror Lake and near Tuolumne Meadows. I also thank those whose donations to the Conservancy made the book possible; their generosity carries on a legacy of philanthropy as old—and as vital—as the national park idea itself.

One of my proudest moments in life was being designated as an honorary park ranger (hat and all!) in 2009. Working on this book reminded me again that the *real* rangers are the ones who deserve to be honored. A number of them provided me with both information and friendship on this project, in the proud tradition of the National Park Service: Dean Shenk, Monica Buhler, Dick Ewart, Shelton Johnson, Julia Parker, Phil Johnson, Woody Smeck, Patty and Don Neubacher. Stephen Mather would be proud of you. I am grateful to you.

Finally I wish to thank Dianne Kearns Duncan, who always encourages me to keep moving forward—on the trail or on a manuscript—and Emme and Will Duncan, *our* seeds of the future.

—DAYTON DUNCAN
WALPOLE, NEW HAMPSHIRE

SELECTED BIBLIOGRAPHY

Badé, William Frederic. *The Life and Letters of John Muir.* New York: Houghton Mifflin Company, 1924.

Bowles, Samuel. *Across the Continent: A Summer's Journey to the Rocky Mountains, the Mormons, and the Pacific States.* Springfield, Massachusetts: Samuel Bowles & Company, 1865.

Brinkley, Douglas. *The Wilderness Warrior: Theodore Roosevelt and the Crusade for America.* New York: HarperCollins Publishers, 2009.

Browning, Peter, ed. *John Muir in His Own Words: A Book of Quotations.* Lafayette, California: Great West Books, 1988.

Bunnell, Lafayette Houghton. *Discovery of the Yosemite and the Indian War of 1851 Which Led to That Event.* Yosemite National Park: Yosemite Association, 1990.

Carr, Ethan. *Wilderness by Design: Landscape Architecture and the National Park Service.* Lincoln: University of Nebraska Press, 1998.

Cutright, Paul Russell. *Theodore Roosevelt: The Making of a Conservationist.* Urbana: University of Illinois Press, 1985.

Duncan, Dayton. *Miles from Nowhere: Tales from America's Contemporary Frontier.* New York: Viking, 1993.

Duncan, Dayton, and Ken Burns. *The National Parks: America's Best Idea.* New York: Alfred A. Knopf, 2011.

Engberg, Robert E. *John Muir Summering in the Sierra.* Madison: University of Wisconsin Press, 1984.

Gifford, Terry, ed. *John Muir: His Life and Letters and Other Writings.* Seattle: The Mountaineers, 1996.

Godfrey, Elizabeth. *Yosemite Indians.* Revised by James Snyder and Craig Bates with the cooperation of The American Indian Council of Mariposa County. Yosemite National Park: Yosemite Association, 1977.

Hampton, H. Duane. *How the U.S. Cavalry Saved Our National Parks.* Bloomington: Indiana University Press, 1971.

Harris, William G. *Lincoln's Last Months.* Cambridge: Harvard University Press, 2004.

Hartesveldt, Richard J., H. Thomas Harvey, Howard S. Shellhammer, and Ronald E. Stecker. *Giant Sequoias.* Fifth edition. Three Rivers, California: Sequoia Natural History Association, 2010.

_____. *The Giant Sequoia of the Sierra.* Nevada, Washington: U.S. Department of the Interior, 1975.

Hollander, Ovando James. *Life of Schuyler Colfax.* New York: Fund & Wagnalls, 1886.

Huntley, Jen A. *The Making of Yosemite: James Mason Hutchings and the Origin of America's Most*

Popular National Park. Lawrence: University Press of Kansas, 2011.

Hurtado, Albert L. *Indian Survival on the California Frontier.* New Haven: Yale University Press, 1988.

Hutchings, J. M. *In the Heart of the Sierras.* Oakland, California: Pacific Press Publishing House, 1886.

_____. *Scenes of Wonder and Curiosity in California.* San Francisco: Hutchings & Rosenfield, Publishers, 1861.

Johnson, Robert Underwood. *Remembered Yesterdays.* Boston: Little, Brown, 1923.

Johnston, Hank. "Glacier Point Tramway." In *Yosemite's Yesterdays.* Yosemite: Flying Spur Press, 1989.

_____. *Ho! For Yo-Semite.* El Portal, California: Yosemite Association, 2000.

_____. "Yosemite's Four (almost five) 'Inspiration Points.'" *Yosemite* 59, no. 4 (Fall 1997).

_____. *The Yosemite Grant, 1864–1906.* Yosemite National Park: Yosemite Association, 1995.

Jones, Holway R. *John Muir and the Sierra Club: The Battle for Yosemite.* San Francisco: The Sierra Club, 1965.

Kimes, William F. "With Theodore Roosevelt and John Muir in Yosemite." *Brand Book Number 14.* Los Angeles Corral, 1974.

Kruska, Dennis. *James Mason Hutchings of Yo Semite: A Biography and Bibliography.* San Francisco: The Book Club of California, 2009.

La Pena, Frank, Craig D. Bates, and Steven P. Medley, eds. *Legends of the Yosemite Miwok.* Yosemite National Park: Yosemite Association, 1993.

Leidig, Charles. "Charlie Leidig's Report of President Roosevelt's Visit in May, 1903." Manuscript. Yosemite National Park Library.

Ludlow, Fitz Hugh. *The Heart of the Continent: A Record of Travel across the Plains and in Oregon.* New York: Hurd and Houghton, 1871.

Martin, Justin. *Genius of Place: The Life of Frederick Law Olmsted.* Philadelphia: Da Capo Press, 2011.

Meyerson, Harvey. *Nature's Army: When Soldiers Fought for Yosemite.* Lawrence: University Press of Kansas, 2001.

Muir, John. *My First Summer in the Sierra.* One-hundredth anniversary illustrated edition, with foreword by Dayton Duncan and Ken Burns. New York: Houghton Mifflin Harcourt, 2011.

_____. *Our National Parks.* Boston: Houghton Mifflin Company, 1901.

_____. *The Yosemite.* New York: The Century Co., 1912.

Olmsted, Frederick Law. *Yosemite and the Mariposa Grove: A Preliminary Report, 1865.* Yosemite National Park: Yosemite Association, 2009.

Palmquist, Peter E. *Carleton E. Watkins: Photographer of the American West.* Albuquerque: University of New Mexico Press, 1983.

Ranney, Victoria Post, ed. *The Papers of Frederick Law Olmsted.* Baltimore: Johns Hopkins University Press, 1990.

Rawls, James C. *Indians of California.* Norman: University of Oklahoma Press, 1984.

Richardson, Albert D. *Beyond the Mississippi: From the Great River to the Great Ocean.* Hartford, Connecticut: N.p., 1867.

Roper, Laura Wood. *FLO: A Biography of Frederick Law Olmsted.* Baltimore: Johns Hopkins University Press, 1973.

Runte, Alfred. *Yosemite: The Embattled Wilderness.* Lincoln: University of Nebraska Press, 1990.

Russell, Carl Parcher. *One Hundred Years in Yosemite.* Yosemite National Park: Yosemite Association, 1992.

Sanborn, Margaret. *Yosemite: Its Discovery, Its Wonders, and Its People.* Yosemite National Park: Yosemite Association, 1989.

Sargent, Shirley. *Galen Clark: Yosemite Guardian.* Revised fourth edition. Yosemite: Flying Spur Press, 2001.

_____. *John Muir in Yosemite.* Revised third edition. Yosemite: Flying Spur Press, 2000.

Sellars, Richard West. *Preserving Nature in the National Parks.* New Haven: Yale University Press, 1997.

Spence, Mark David. *Dispossessing the Wilderness: Indian Removal and the Making of the National Parks.* Oxford: Oxford University Press, 1999.

Taylor, Mrs. H. J. "The Return of the Last Survivor." *University of California Chronicle* (January 1931).

Teale, Edwin Way. *The Wilderness World of John Muir.* Boston: Houghton Mifflin Company, 1954.

Thayer, James Bradley. *A Western Journey with Mr. Emerson.* San Francisco: The Book Club of California, 1980.

Thoreau, Henry David. *The Maine Woods.* New York: Penguin Books, 1988.

Turner, Frederick. *Rediscovering America: John Muir in His Time and Ours.* New York: Viking Penguin Inc., 1985.

Ward, Geoffrey C. *The West: An Illustrated History.* Boston: Little, Brown and Company, 1996.

Wolfe, Linnie Marsh. *John of the Mountains: The Unpublished Journals of John Muir.* Madison: University of Wisconsin Press, 1938.

_____. *Son of the Wilderness: The Life of John Muir.* Madison: University of Wisconsin Press, 2003.

Worster, Donald. *A Passion for Nature: The Life of John Muir.* Oxford: Oxford University Press, 2008.

IMAGE CREDITS

76: Library of Congress, Manuscript Division

84, 133: Hank Johnston Collection

88, 92, 93, 95, 97, 100, 118, 119, 143, 153: John Muir Papers, Holt-Atherton Special Collections, University of the Pacific Library. © 1984 Muir-Hanna Trust

89: Wisconsin Historical Society, WHS-4954

99: Photography Collection, Miriam and Ira D. Wallach Division of Art, Prints and Photographs, The New York Public Library, Astor, Lenox and Tilden Foundations

108: Image courtesy of History Colorado, William Henry Jackson Collection, Scan #20103951

121: University of Washington Libraries Special Collections, Arthur Churchill Warner Collection, PH Coll 273

131: Montana Historical Society Research Center, Archives, H-3012

135: Print Collection, Miriam and Ira D. Wallach Division of Art, Prints and Photographs, The New York Public Library, Astor, Lenox and Tilden Foundations

137: Burton Historical Collection, Detroit Public Library

140: Image #42131, American Museum of Natural History Library

146: Virtual Steam Car Museum, Inc. Donald & Carolyn Hoke Collection. virtualsteamcarmuseum.org

150: © Charles Cramer

157, 170: National Park Service Historic Photograph Collection

163: Courtesy of the California State Library

171 (left): National Park Service Historic Photograph Collection/photographer Carl Parcher Russell

171 (right): Photo: Cedric Wright, courtesy of the Colby Memorial Library, Sierra Club

173: © The Ansel Adams Publishing Rights Trust, licensed by Corbis Corporation

178: private collection

182: National Park Service photo by Susan Michael

183 (left): courtesy of Monica Buhler

183 (right): courtesy of Dick Ewart

184: photo: Amy Fronczkiewicz; courtesy Yosemite National Park Archives: Slide Collection, YOSE-06815

185: photo: Aline Allen, courtesy of Yosemite Conservancy

187, 188, 190: photo: Keith S. Walklet, courtesy of Yosemite Conservancy

INDEX

ABOUT THE AUTHOR

DAYTON DUNCAN is an award-winning writer and documentary filmmaker. He has served on the boards of the National Park Foundation, the Student Conservation Association and the Conservation Lands Foundation and was appointed by President Clinton as chair of the American Heritage Rivers Advisory Commission. For more than twenty years he has been making documentaries for PBS with Ken Burns, including *The National Parks: America's Best Idea*, for which he won two Emmy awards as writer and producer and was named honorary park ranger by the director of the National Park Service. This is his twelfth book.